PRAXIS

BEYOND THEORY

GABRIEL ETZEL *and* BEN GUTIERREZ

Praxis: Beyond Theory
Copyright © 2012 by Gabriel Etzel and Ben Gutierrez

Permissions Department
Academx Publishing Services, Inc.

P.O. Box 56527
Virgina Beach, VA 23456
Printed in the United States of America

ISBN (10): 1-60036-535-3
ISBN (13): 978-1-60036-535-5

DEDICATION

TO THE EXCEPTIONAL STUDENTS OF LIBERTY UNIVERSITY—

You sharpen our thinking with your valuable insights,

You energize us with your enthusiasm for life,

You humble us by your commitment to Christ.

YOU ARE THE FINEST STUDENTS IN THE WORLD!

THERE IS NO BETTER PLACE TO TEACH THAN AT
LIBERTY UNIVERSITY!

ACKNOWLEDGMENTS

This page serves to recognize the myriad of support we received in writing this book. Without their help, we would not have been able to complete this very satisfying task.

Thank you to our wives Whitney Etzel and Tammy Gutierrez, whose support and encouragement through the ups and downs of life keep us going and enthused to continue to minister.

Thank you to our precious children, Landon Etzel, Ava Etzel, Isaac Etzel, Lauren Gutierrez, and Emma Gutierrez. You fill our lives with such joy and laughter. Our prayer is that every day we will live out before you the truths taught in this book. We love you so much.

To Jill Walker, your acute attention to detail in managing the editing process of this book has been unparalleled. Your professionalism, knowledge of the process, and flexible spirit have been the most critical factors in finishing this book. Without your contribution, this book could not have been completed. Many thanks!

To Anne Alexander, thank you for paying attention to the smallest of details. Your technical editing improved the overall readability of the book and added the finishing touches to the manuscript. Anne can be contacted for writing and editing projects through WordWise, LLC at annea2@bellsouth.net.

To Russell Shaw, thank you for your ability to take words and bring them to life through the art of illustration. Your creativity and devotion to detail have made the finishing touches to this project possible. Russell can be contacted through his website www.russellshawblog.com.

To our leadership and colleagues of Liberty University, thank you for your encouragement to write, teach, administrate, lead and dream big. You provide us with the richest environments within which to edify the Body of Christ. There is no better place to live, work, and minister than on Liberty Mountain!

TABLE OF CONTENTS

FORMULATING A SYSTEMATIC THEOLOGY

THE BIBLE

MANKIND/SIN

JESUS CHRIST

SALVATION

THE CHURCH

THE CHRISTIAN LIFE

END TIMES

INTRODUCTION:
THEOLOGY MUST WORK IN REAL LIFE

"Being proud about giving a lecture on theology that is devoid of any specific, practical and relevant application to a person's life is like being proud of a barren tree."
- BEN GUTIERREZ

"This is way over my head!"

"So what? Why bother? You can't understand any of it anyways."

"Theology is only for a chosen few with minds who can handle all that information."

"Can we just forget talking about all this theology and just talk about Jesus?"

"You don't need to be a theologian in order to worship God!"

We've heard it for too long

We have heard all these responses (and more) from people who have decided not to continue to study theology or engage in theological discussions—and it's unfortunate. The regrettable thing about this is they are declaring something that is so beautiful, useful and spiritually profitable to be utterly unnecessary. It ought not to be this way.

Teaching theology is incomplete without also teaching how it can change someone's life! We believe that theology lacks effectiveness unless it produces life-change within the human heart, which translates into changed actions! So many professors have taught theology as if it were a huge list of terms, definitions and concepts that have to be memorized—without ever taking the students one step further and teaching them how theology can affect their lives, speech and efforts today. The purpose of this book is to aid you in understanding both the basic concepts of the Christian faith as well as how you can practically live out these basic concepts in your life . . . now . . . today!

We believe that the ultimate thrill for any theology professor ought to be the observation of a student actually allowing their theological beliefs to affect their daily actions and decisions! The problem is, there are too many theologians who are more interested in hearing themselves speak than in seeing life-change in their students. Rather than focusing on covering all of the topics for the day within the allotted class time, we believe it's more important for the truths that we study in theology to influence and shape every decision a believer makes—in real life, in real time.

If no one can understand how to live out the theological truth, then all we have accomplished is to bring some false sense of satisfaction to a theology lecturer who enjoyed hearing himself blabber words for an hour-long lecture. Or we've given a theological author some sort of gratification from writing voluminous amounts of glib and perfunctory erudition (spoken like a true theologian, huh?).

Be sure to add water

Teaching theology without making specific, practical and relevant application to one's life is like making hot chocolate by pouring the chocolate powder in a mug but never adding water! Sure, you "technically" have the right hot chocolate ingredient , but the problem is you lack the desired consistency that makes a cup of hot chocolate truly satisfying! It is not until you add the "water" (i.e., practical application) that you have the right mixture and consistency that makes theology purposeful. To avoid this necessary mixture is to resemble one who has never really grasped the genuine meaning of the truth—James 2:14a, 17, 20 touches on this idea:

"What good is it, dear brothers and sisters, if you say you have faith but don't show it by your actions? . . . So you see, faith by itself isn't enough. Unless it produces good deeds, it is dead and useless. How foolish! Can't you see that faith without good deeds is useless?"

You will resemble what you deeply believe

Have you ever heard the phrase, "You are what you eat?" Well, the same applies to theology, "You will act upon what you deeply believe!" Or, as the Bible puts it, "What you say flows from what is in your heart" (Luke 6:45b). There is no getting around the reality that actions are based upon a foundation of thoughts, beliefs and convictions. What you believe will affect your words, actions and reactions in life. Therefore, it is important to both know what you believe and make sure your actions are aligned with your beliefs.

We have a conviction

We believe that if you are going to discuss theology you must be intensely practical. We believe that if you go diving deep in the waters of theological discussion, the more specific and profound your personal applications should be. The deeper the theological discussion, the more intentionally practical the outcome should be. That's why this basic theology book is unapologetically practical.

We want you to hold these same convictions. We don't want you to be satisfied with simply gaining knowledge, but that you strain yourselves to whatever degree necessary to learn how to apply any and all theological concepts to your life, prior to declaring mastery of a theological concept.

This book is unapologetically practical!
We believe that if you, the student, are able to simply read and understand a theological concept, but you are unable to know how it should affect your actions—your knowledge is incomplete and there has been a failure to accurately instruct. That's why we are committed to supplement all of the theological writings that are available to students today with this brief, concise book on making theology relevant.

Keep it simple
In order to make theology practical and relevant, we believe that you have to talk in clear and simple terms. This is not to say that you have to "dumb down" the teaching—not at all. What we are saying is that we believe that "theology" doesn't have to be a synonym for "confusion" after five minutes of reading a textbook about theology. We believe that profound theological truths can indeed be conveyed in simple, understandable terms for most everyone to understand. We will not dismiss theology for practice, but rather harmonize theology and practice. That is how we have written this book.

We don't have all the answers
This book is intended to accompany any larger theological textbook with the specific goal to provide practical, relevant application to any theological lesson. We readily admit that we don't have all the answers. We also do not want to claim that this book will cover every important theological doctrine. We understand that there are many important theological doctrines that are not addressed in this book. That's why we encourage you to consult other evangelical Christian authors who may have elaborated more thoroughly on these doctrines and covered some teachings that we were unable to address in this book. Again, our goal is to focus on briefly summarizing several theological doctrines and describing the practical implications of each one. We beg your forgiveness if we have not addressed a theological doctrine that is important to you. The omission of any major doctrine is not a statement in any way regarding the importance of that particular doctrine.

Don't feel intimidated
Prior to reading this book, you may never have encountered the study of theology before—let alone considered how theology could apply to your own personal life. I want to encourage you that you are not alone. We remember how it was to engage some of these concepts for the first time. Collectively, we have talked to hundreds of students who have asked us the same kind of questions—questions with which we ourselves have grappled.

So we have committed to remain mindful of what you are possibly feeling and thinking as you review each one of these theological concepts.

We say everything out of love

In writing this book, we strived to keep it real, relevant and respectful. We were cautious not to sound too demeaning or disrespectful. We attempted not to include any "preachy" talk that may sound good but is irrelevant to one's daily life. In addition, we have made every attempt in our summary and application of each theological doctrine to display the sincerest respect to those who have not yet placed their faith in Jesus Christ as their Lord and Savior. Please accept our sincerest apologies if you feel that we have not accomplished this goal, or if we come across as being disrespectful in any way. While it is true that we do not hide the fact that we believe the doctrines presented in this book, we have endeavored to present our thoughts respectfully to you.

You are on our mind

Our sincerest wish for you is that throughout this journey with us you will discover wonderful truths about (1) God as the Creator of the world, (2) the life and death and resurrection of Jesus Christ, (3) the daily guidance provided by the Holy Spirit, (4) life, death and eternity, (5) your need to be forgiven by a loving God Who invited you to know Him intimately. We will do all we can to make sure that the major questions you have are addressed in a respectful and honest manner.

We will pray for you during this journey!

While there is no way we could possibly meet every person who reads this book (even though we would like to!), we promise to pray regularly for you that you will "grow in the grace and knowledge of the Lord Jesus Christ" (2 Peter 3:18). With every page you read, we hope you will remember that you have been and are being prayed for by us and many others. So, take this season of your life to really engage the critical questions that you have always wanted to search out. Use this time to do some real soul-searching. We will pray that God will surprise all of us by how much He will teach us on this journey!

Sincerely,

— GABRIEL ETZEL *and* BEN GUTIERREZ

FORMULATING A
SYSTEMATIC THEOLOGY

THEOLOGY

(THEE-OL-UH-JEE)

"That discipline which strives to give a coherent statement of the doctrines of the Christian faith, based primarily on the Scriptures, placed in the context of culture in general, worded in a contemporary idiom, and related to the issues of life."
- MILLARD ERICKSON, *Christian Theology*, 23

It has been said that everyone is a theologian, because everyone has thoughts about God. At its core, that statement is true of everyone who has ever lived, because we all have thoughts and ideas about God. What is more, we all act on these thoughts in the way we live our lives. Our view of God influences the way we live out our lives. If we think God is "the old man upstairs," then we tend to live our life as though He will not hold us accountable for what we do, or perhaps He doesn't even pay attention to what we are doing. Others view God much like a mean kid who is waiting for us to make a mistake so He can punish us.

It was A.W. Tozer who stated, "The low view of God entertained almost universally among Christians is the cause of a hundred lesser evils everywhere among us. A whole new philosophy of the Christian life has resulted from this one basic error in our religious thinking" (The Knowledge of the Holy: The Attributes of God, vii). It is because of this truth that the study of theology is so important. The way we see God influences everything we do in life—the way we treat each other (as individuals being created in God's image), our stewardship of God's creation, our understanding of our vocation as a way to glorify God—all areas of life are changed as our view of God changes.

In his chapter on the church's role in apologetics, author and speaker Ravi Zacharias makes the following statement, "C.S. Lewis once stated that if you cannot explain a simple truth, chances are that you do not understand it yourself. In my own journey into apologetics, I recall spending many a morning run or walk asking myself if I trusted my own answers. How convincing were they to me? But then came a second question: do I really understand the depth of the questions that are being raised? That is what took me onto the long road of training." (Beyond Opinion, 313).

We are faced with questions about God every day. Some of these questions we ask of ourselves, some of these questions are asked by our co-workers, or our spouses, or our children. God has given us a responsibility to speak to the hope that we have within us (see 1 Peter 3:15). Peter wrote those words in the context of an individual suffering for doing what is right. As others see that individual living for God, even in the midst of unsubstantiated suffering, they will want to know how it is that the person continues to do right. Peter says that in those instances, we need to be ready to give an answer.

I strongly believe that unless you have determined before you enter a difficult situation why you want to be faithful to God, then the answer may not come to you in that stressful moment. Let's obey God's command to be ready to share the hope that we have.

PRACTICAL APPLICATION:

A "theo-what?!"

Friend – Best-man – Father – Husband – Son – Professor – Lecturer – Author

All of these titles describe me—and I am not surprised by any of them. In fact, growing up, I prayed to God for some of these titles to be true of me. I always enjoyed teaching. I wanted to get married someday. And even though in my high school and early college years it took me a while to warm up to the idea of children in my life, I eventually welcomed the title of "father." But never did I anticipate being called a "theologian."

I don't have the "look"
I always thought that "theologians" were older men who grew unkempt beards (for some reason, every smart guy in my mind has a beard) and wore a semi-wrinkled, button-down-collar shirt underneath a sports coat with elbow patches. I though this term was applied to those who had no idea who the short stop for the New York Yankees was in the current season, they but could describe for you every worn portion of ancient parchment that is currently preserving the ancient biblical writings of the Old Testament book of Habakkuk – that was a theologian to me.

Add that to your vita
But while you may never take off work to observe ancient third century codex of the Gospel of Luke in the Smithsonian (which really exists, by the way!), that does not mean you aren't a theologian. Whether you are: (1) An informed theologian—have researched pertinent information, deliberated upon it, and have come to conclusions; (2) A theologian-in process—developing in your position with a sincere desire to make the right conclusions; (3) An uninformed theologian—either you never have taken the time to research pertinent information, or you willingly have chosen not to research pertinent information. Whichever path you've chosen, to some degree you are a theologian. The good news is that everyone has the right to jump into

conversations regarding spiritual things.

What you believe (or deny) will dictate how you live
To whatever level you hold a position on spiritual issues, you will undoubt-edly allow what you believe to affect your actions. For example, if you have never considered the biblical teachings regarding the eternal state of a person's soul, then you will not necessarily see the value of researching the biblical writings that teach about a person's need to have peace with God. However, just because you do not engage with the question of the eternal state of one's soul does not mean that you do not have a position on the matter. Your position is simply that it is not important for someone to have the answer to this question in their lifetime.

Whereas someone else who has pondered the biblical teachings on the fact that one's soul is eternal and has contemplated the question of whether to accept Jesus Christ as their personal Savior, this person has determined that this particular spiritual question has value and should play a profound role in our thinking during this lifetime. So regardless of how passionate or unemotional you are about spiritual issues, you are living ac-cording to some view of theology.

Will I like what I discover?
Why don't people like to consider spiritual questions? There are tons of reasons to be sure, but I have found that some people simply do not wish to study spiritual questions because of the implications of the answers upon their lives. In other words, they feel that if serious consideration is given to some of these profound questions of life and God, then they may learn that they have a responsibility to respond accordingly (and they would be correct). Thus, they choose not to engage in spiritual discussion. But ignoring the spiritual questions doesn't negate the responsibility to be a good theologian. Remember this principle: One's inactivity does not release a person from being a responsible theologian.

Start your journey today
I encourage you to begin this spiritual journey today. Take time to reflect on spiritual questions—and ask a lot of questions yourself. Take time to engage other Christians in conversations regarding these important spiritual issues. Be excited about what you may find. But most importantly, insist that you will respond to the truth that you discover during this spiritual journey. Commit to obeying what you learn about God, and what He says about your life and your relationship to Him.

It can be an exciting journey.

The fact is you are already laying a foundation . . . so you might as well make sure that you are building it on solid ground.

Study what the Bible says about the importance of studying theology
Here are some more verses to read on this topic — Psalm 46:10; Matthew
22:29; John 5:39-40; 2 Timothy 2:15.

Write it down... ↴

...& make it HAPPEN!

FAITH

(FEYTH)

"Question: What is faith in Jesus Christ? Answer: Faith in Jesus Christ is a saving grace, whereby we receive and rest upon him alone for salvation, as he is offered to us in the gospel."
- WESTMINSTER SHORTER CATECHISM

The Greek word for faith is the word, pistis, which means the conviction that something is true. For the purposes of our discussion here we will focus on the saving faith in Jesus. If understood correctly, faith applies not just to the moment of salvation, but to the entire life of the person from the moment of conversion. As Wayne Grudem states, "Saving faith is trust in Jesus Christ as a living person for forgiveness of sins and eternal life with God" (Bible Doctrine, 308).

A couple of important factors should be remembered as we think about the significance of faith. First, we are saved by faith alone. Ephesians 2:8-9 makes this very clear. Paul says that "God saved you by his grace when you believed. And you can't take credit for this; it is a gift from God. Salvation is not a reward for the good things we have done, so none of us can boast about it." We do not earn our way to God. We do not work our way to heaven. When we were still in our sins, a rebel of the Kingdom of God, Jesus died for our sins (Romans 5:8). Second, faith without works is dead. James 2:17 indicates, "So you see, faith by itself isn't enough. Unless it produces good deeds, it is dead and useless." True faith in Jesus Christ will bring about a change in the life of the person. Paul speaks to this change as putting off the old man and putting on the new self (Ephesians 4:17-24). Theologically the term regeneration is used to identify this new birth. If a person is truly saved, he will show it in the way he lives his life.

At this point some may be a little confused, because it may seem as though two different things are being said: (1) It is all about faith without works, and (2) Faith has works. Contrary to what some may suggest, I believe the two concepts fit together nicely, as long as we have the proper understanding of each concept. The idea of faith alone without works speaks directly to the conversion of the individual. Does works save the person? No, only faith saves the person, which is a free gift from God. So, why does James mention works? The answer is that James is referring to the evidence of that faith. James is saying that if you really have saving faith, then you will show that by the changed life that you live. You will show it by your actions.

Another important thing to keep in mind is Jesus said that even a little faith could accomplish great things (Luke 17:6). As significant as it is to have faith, it is essential to make sure you have faith in the right object or person. Perhaps you have had a conviction that something is true in the past, only to find out that you were wrong. Even though you had faith, that faith was ultimately only as good as the object or person it was placed in. Concerning putting our faith in Jesus, we have good reason to place our trust in Him. He has demonstrated Himself faithful in the past, and promises to remember His followers when He enters His Kingdom (John 14). Ultimately Jesus showed that He is worthy of our faith when He was raised from the dead. That miraculous event should solidify in your mind the credibility of Jesus.

PRACTICAL APPLICATION:

Nice try but not quite

There have been many attempts at explaining the "faith" in the life of a believer. Unfortunately, many of them fall apart at some level or worse yet, never began with a correct premise and understanding of faith in the first place. A few of them come to mind and need to be scrutinized to demonstrate that these analogies fall apart at some point (or never get off the ground)! We do not want you to be confused as you build your own faith in the Lord Jesus Christ.

"Blind faith" doesn't work

I am always taken back by Christians who claim to have "blind faith" in the Lord and that there is "no way to prove that their faith is true or not—they just have chosen to have faith in Jesus Christ." To make such a claim is to ignore the God-given intellect and reason that He infused within us at the moment of creation in order for us to discern truth that is provided through His Word, the Bible (see the chapters on "Reason and Intellect," "Language," "The Bible," and "Truth").

The "chair" could fall over

Many well intentioned believers offer another commonly shared analogy that unfortunately falls short when explaining the necessary faith that a person must have in order to become a believer in Jesus Christ. I have heard some believers pull up a folding chair on stage and begin to describe how sitting in the chair is like having faith in Jesus Christ—you don' t think about it, you just do it—and you simply have faith that the chair will hold you up.

This analogy is okay to explain the initial confidence level that you can place in Christ—but only once you have determined that the chair is constructed soundly and able to sustain you when you sit on it. A problem with this analogy enters when you ask the question, "So, that chair might hold me up today . . . and maybe tomorrow, but what about after that metal folding chair is left out in the rain for a few years? Can I trust it to hold me when it's rusted and corroded? Or, what about a brand new chair holding up a person that exceeds the weight capacity? This analogy may do well at illustrating how to rest confidently in something after you have considered its claims to support you are truly trustworthy, but faith as a whole is much more than an unexamined faith.

Say it plainly
I have found that the best way to explain how to have true faith in Jesus Christ is to say it plainly, without analogies. Simply stating the facts that must be known and believed upon is the best way to explain the historical and factual nature of the level of faith required of Christianity.

Here it goes:

God Himself entered into the world to offer His own life as a payment for the sin caused by mankind's choice to disobey God at the beginning of creation (see the chapter on "The Virgin Birth"). After Jesus gave His life on a cross, He physically rose again three days later (see the chapters on "Atonement" and "Resurrection"). His resurrection proved that all He said about offering forgiveness for sins was not only possible, but it was a sure promise. Before Jesus ascended back into heaven (see the chapter on "Ascension"), He instructed His followers to share the good news about how a person can be saved from the sin that every person has resident within him/her (see the chapters on "Sin" and "Salvation"). In order to be "saved" each person must trust the historical facts that: (1) Jesus was indeed God incarnate (i.e. in the flesh), devoid of any sin in His being; (2) He literally came to earth; (3) He offered forgiveness of sin through His atoning sacrifice on the cross (see the chapter on "Atonement"); (4) He physically rose again from the dead (see the chapter on "Resurrection"); (5) He is the only sufficient payment able to forgive mankind's sinfulness. Then, having accepted responsibility for your own sinfulness, ask God to forgive you and become the Savior of your soul.

The Result
When you accept these facts along with placing your trust and dependence upon Jesus Christ alone, you become a member of His family. And after you have experienced the proven reality that God can save your soul, you should have great confidence in believing Him to help you with the

FAITH IN JESUS IS NEVER A BLIND FAITH . . . NEVER A TEMPORARY, UNCERTAIN FAITH. IT IS A CERTAIN, CONFIDENT FAITH IN A PERSON—IN GOD HIMSELF, JESUS CHRIST.

day-to-day things in your life because He has demonstrated His trustworthiness in providing you a secure salvation.

So, as a believer when someone may hear me so easily say, "I am trusting God for this/that," it is because God is a trustworthy promise-maker and keeper that has both proven His power and authority in my life. Faith in Jesus is never a blind faith . . . never a temporary, uncertain faith. It is a certain, confident faith in a person—in God Himself, Jesus Christ.

Study what the Bible says about the importance of faith
Here are some more verses to read on this topic — Genesis 12; Hebrews 11; Ephesians 2:4-10; James 2:14-26; Romans 10:17.

Write it down... ↘

...& make it
HAPPEN!

REASON/INTELLECT

(IN-TL-EKT)

"The capacity of the human intellect to carry out organized mental activity such as the association of ideas, induction and deduction of inferences, or formulation of value judgments."
- EVANGELICAL DICTIONARY OF THEOLOGY, 990

Is there a place for human reason in the study of theology? Absolutely. In fact, by even asking the question one has entered into an exercise of reason to some degree. It seems impossible to imagine a legitimate theological system that doesn't utilize reason in some form. Although some systems have tried to avoid the use of reason, if they attempt to convince others of their views, then they have just shown the flaw in their own understanding.

God says in Isaiah 1:18, "Come now, let's settle this . . ." The NKJV translates this passage, "Come now, let us reason together . . ." The Hebrew word used in the passage is, yakach, and carries within it the understanding of judging, proving, or deciding. Elsewhere in the Bible the use of reason is also encouraged as the prophets remind the people of Israel to remember the lessons they have learned from the past about God's faithfulness. Within the New Testament, the martyrdom of Stephen is another example. When he is before the Sanhedrin he provides a history of the nation of Israel to demonstrate the person and work of Jesus (Acts 7).

Recognizing the use of reason is not an attempt to downplay the significance of the effect of sin on all of humanity. Romans 1 makes it clear that sin has affected our minds. Without the renewing of the mind by the Holy Spirit we are without hope of understanding the things of God (Romans 12:2). God makes it clear that His ways are higher than our ways, and His thoughts are higher than our thoughts (Isaiah 55:8). However, we do have the Holy Spirit, and we do have the testimony of the Word of God, and we do have the words and the work of Jesus to assist us as we process through God's truth in both His general and His special revelation.

Throughout the Bible we see the writers of Scripture making arguments from the text, from creation, and from history. Jesus did this at times throughout His ministry. He appeals to the entirety of the individual, which includes the individual's mental capacities. This does not by any means indicate that we should place our own human understanding above God or His Word. My statements are simply an attempt to show that reason is appealed to in Scripture.

The history of the Christian church is varied when it comes to the topic of reason. Some see little place for the use of reason in the Christian faith. Others emphasize it to the point of nearly elevating it to a place equal to, or above, Scripture itself. As is the challenge with many principles concerning theology, it is important that we do not place anyone or anything in God's rightful place of supremacy. Reason is a very powerful tool which God has given us. Our job is to use it for His glory and not our own.

" NEVER ONCE DOES THE BIBLE OR CHRISTI-ANITY REQUIRE BELIEVERS TO DIVORCE THEM-SELVES FROM THE GOD-GIVEN ABILITY TO THINK CRITICALLY AS THEY ENGAGE IN THE STUDY OF TRUTH. "

PRACTICAL APPLICATION:

Don't check your brain at the door

Never once does the Bible or Christianity require believers to divorce themselves from the God-given ability to think critically as they engage in the study of truth. God has created human beings with an exceptional ability to think, feel and process truth (see the chapter on the "Image of God"). So of course God welcomes us to engage His truth with our minds and hearts. Jesus Himself said, "'You must love the LORD your God with all your heart, all your soul, and all your mind'" (Matthew 22:37). In the book Consider the following examples are provided that serve as helpful reminders that "critical thinking" is both acceptable and expected when discussing spiritual issues:

> Just as we often have to set aside our passion in order to think clearly, to think critically, in order to make wise decisions. It is a common practice we do every day, but we may never even be aware of it.

> For example, in the English language, how do you know whether the word "r-e-a-d" should be understood as a directive to "read a book," or if it is to be understood as a past-tense word describing a moment that someone "had already read that book last week?"

> Critical thinking.

> Another example is with the word "conflict." Do we have a "conflict" (i.e., a moment of tense disagreement) occurring between our children? Or, does our view "conflict" with another's view (i.e., to be contradictory, used as a verb)? How do we know the difference?

Critical thinking.

What is the difference between "supervision" and "oversight?" Break those two words apart (super-vision and over-sight) and you have "super" correlating with the word "over," and you have "vision" looking pretty similar to the word "sight." But I think you would agree that there is a difference between someone who has supervision over employees and a big sister who simply has oversight of her siblings while Mom or Dad is on the phone. How can you distinguish the difference?

Critical thinking.

In each of the examples above, understanding the context is necessary in the process of critical thinking. Discernment is needed in every area of our lives, but the path to discernment is through critical thinking.

Some in American culture even reject the idea of questioning what another person believes by championing the idea of tolerance and pluralism. What a person believes is important and being able to critically think and to intelligently challenge incorrect thinking is essential in the process of making wise decisions in life.

Give it some thought
When considering the truth claims of Christianity, take some time to reason with a believer over the statements and implications of the claims. Take some time to think it over as the repercussions will affect both your life while upon this earth and beyond. Take time to engage the discussion with someone who will talk it out with you. Raise questions and approach a professor, classmate, or friend that you know is a believer and will commit to join you in these discussions. Of course, no one person will have all the answers, so find someone who will be honest enough to admit that he/she doesn't have all the answers but will promise you to search the Bible and approach other believers in order help.

It is a worthwhile journey to take
I want to encourage you to commit to begin a spiritual journey for truth over the next few weeks. It can both stimulate your intellectual desire for truth and stir your emotions and passions as you experience life-changing realities. And if you open yourself up to what God wants to teach you through the Bible, it will change your life forever.

Study what the Bible says about the role of reason and intellect in Christianity
Here are some more verses to read on this topic—Isaiah 1:18; Romans 12:2; Proverbs 1-3; Acts 17:2-3, 18:4.

Write it down... ↘

...& make it
HAPPEN!

LANGUAGE

(LANG-GWIJ)

"'My thoughts are nothing like your thoughts,' says the LORD. 'And
my ways are far beyond anything you could imagine. For just as
the heavens are higher than the earth, so my ways are higher than
your ways and my thoughts higher than your thoughts.'"
- ISAIAH 55:8-9

Think for a moment of the power of language. Think of the words we
use that have the potential to have great meaning, but at times are used
flippantly and stripped of meaning. The word "love" is an example of this
concept. I love sports, I love pizza, I love warm weather, but that is different
than my love for my wife and kids. James 3:1-12 speaks to the significance
of the tongue. James mentions the all too often dichotomy between blessing God and cursing others with the same tongue. Truly the words we use
carry great significance.

For the purposes of our discussion here it is important to think through
both the advantages and the limitations of language. We use language all
the time to communicate meaning and truth. I am sitting at my computer in
my house as I write these words, and months (or even years) later you are
reading these words. I hope and pray that I am effectively communicating
to you through this process, and I pray even now that you are hearing from
God in the pages of this book. This is part of the greatness of language. We
can communicate meaning to one another.

However, there are many limitations to the use of language. I remember
being asked in a pre-marital counseling session to explain why I loved my
fiancé. I don't quite remember what I said, but I am confident that it didn't
accurately communicate my love for her. Now, I realize that is not necessarily a weakness with language itself, but rather, it was more of a weakness
with my ability to effectively use language at that time. But, if you stop and
think about it, how is it that we are to communicate very deep and moving
events and feelings and thoughts? Are we not at times limited in our ability
to communicate? I think the writers of the Bible were at times at a loss for
words when trying to describe deep, virtually unimaginable truths. If you
think I am wrong, then take a minute and explain the Trinity. Okay, now, explain the eternality of God. He has always existed. Even that sentence, "He
has always existed" seems to fall very short of the greatness of the thought
I am trying to convey about an eternal God. I recognize that the Bible is
the inspired Word of God. It is God-breathed, which means the words in
the Bible are the words God wanted to be in the Bible. I am not in any way

trying to challenge that idea; however, I am simply trying to recognize that there are limitations in what we can effectively communicate to one another, especially when it comes to an infinite God.

My challenge to you is to recognize the great blessing we have through the use of language, and also to recognize that there are limitations inherent in language. I am very grateful that God chose to inspire His revelation to us through the use of the writers of Scripture. He chose to use limited humanity to communicate something about His infinite self, and that to me is truly amazing.

PRACTICAL APPLICATION:

What does this word mean?

I am commonly asked about different words used in the Bible. Usually, if there is a challenge understanding a term it is because the reader is seeing a word that meant something slightly different when the Bible was written 2000 years ago. The good thing is that there are study tools, research websites, etc., that can assist a reader in gaining the correct understanding for particular words in the Bible. It can be very rewarding to study the chapters, paragraphs, sentences, and words of the Bible.

Be grateful for the words

The first thing I encourage the inquiring person to do is to be grateful that God's Word was delivered to us in a known dialect. God didn't just draft His instruction for life to us in an unintelligible language that humankind was unable to understand. Rather, God actually chose a specific language in a specific season of human history by which to deliver His truth to us. For example, the New Testament was written in first century Koine (COIN-nay) Greek. It was a very common, simple Greek that resembled the vernacular (common speech) of those living in the first century. So, if we want to more clearly understand the meaning of a word in the Bible, we are able to trace the meaning of the word back to the original Koine Greek word. The point being, amid all of the discussions about the meaning of the words and the various nuances of certain words, we ought to be thankful that we are actually able to discuss the meanings of the words found in the Bible rather than wishing it was possible to understand it.

Take time to consider the words

Knowing that we hold God's literal words to all humankind in our hands in the form of the Bible, you ought to take some time to read it and process its teachings. You do not have to be a scholar in order to understand the essential teaching of the Bible. So, jump in and start reading. If you want to learn more about Jesus Christ, why not begin reading the Gospel of John in the New Testament. If you are already a believer and you want to deepen your spiritual understanding of the need for unity within the family of believers, why not begin reading the Letter to the Philippians. If you are curious about the society and the culture in which the Bible was written, why don't you do a search for a resource that provides insights on the manners and customs of the Bible (see the chapter on "Interpretation" for more discussion on useful resources in studying the Bible).

> **KNOWING THAT WE HOLD GOD'S LITERAL WORDS TO ALL HUMANKIND IN OUR HANDS IN THE FORM OF THE BIBLE, YOU OUGHT TO TAKE SOME TIME TO READ IT AND PROCESS ITS TEACHINGS.**

Start today
But wherever you are in your spiritual journey, pick up the Bible today and just begin reading it. Then grab a friend and ask each other questions about some of the words, phrases and teachings. Pray to God and ask Him to help you further understand the meaning of various verses. God's Word is available to us and more likely than not, it already has been translated in your own language. So take advantage of the time and opportunity to hear from God through His Word.

Study what the Bible says about the importance and the impact of language
Here are some more verses to read on this topic—Isaiah 55:8-9; James 3:1-12; Genesis 11:1-9; Romans 8:26.

Write it down... ↘

...& make it
HAPPEN!

TRUTH

(TROOTH)

> "The word truth denotes something that conforms to actuality, is faithful to a standard, or involves sincerity or integrity. The ground for truth is reality itself."
> - EVANGELICAL DICTIONARY OF THEOLOGY, 1219

Standing before Pilate just hours before His crucifixion, Jesus is asked the question, "What is truth" (John 18:38)? It was just hours before this trial, when Jesus was praying in the Garden of Gethsemane prior to His arrest, that Jesus answered the question. He was praying for His disciples during this portion of the prayer, and He asks that the Father, "Make them holy by your truth; teach them your word, which is truth" (John 17:17). Jesus appeals to the Word of God as truth.

It is also interesting to think about conversations Jesus had just after His resurrection, where Jesus speaks of the truth of Scripture. Keep in mind that at the time Jesus is talking, the "Scriptures" that are referred to are the Old Testament writings. The story is recorded in Luke 24, and takes place on a road with two of His followers. In Luke 24:26-27 Jesus says, "'Wasn't it clearly predicted that the Messiah would have to suffer all these things before entering his glory?' Then Jesus took them through the writings of Moses and all the prophets, explaining from all the Scriptures the things concerning himself." Can you imagine Jesus Himself walking you through the Old Testament and explaining the significance of the writings as they related to Him? What an amazing thought to even consider. It is important to keep in mind that we see in this passage that Jesus appeals to the truth of Scripture.

In today's society we talk a lot about truth, but often we have a difficult time coming to conclusions about what the truth really is. Think about all of the debated topics in the media. Is there such a thing as global warming? What are the best economic policies for a nation to practice? The list goes on and on and on. Because each side of the issue has supposed "experts," it could lead some to begin to doubt if there really is an answer. It can cause us to question if there really is truth.

Without trying to oversimplify a very complex conversation, it seems clear from Scripture that truth does exist, and apparently we are able to know and recognize truth (this is what Jesus indicates with His teachings). Although it is sometimes difficult to filter through the many voices speaking to an issue, we should not become discouraged in attempting to find the answer to our questions. Neither should we become antagonistic or agnostic to the existence of truth. Jesus said the Word of God is truth, and that is a great starting point for us.

Jesus also says in John 14:6, "I am the way, the truth, and the life. No one can come to the Father except through me." The word for truth used in the verse is, alētheia, which translated can mean something that is associated with fact or reality. The questions we must ask ourselves relate to our understanding of the existence of truth and also the ability of humanity to grasp truth. Jesus believes that truth exists, and that we can know truth because Jesus teaches that God's Word is truth, and that He is the truth.

PRACTICAL APPLICATION:

I've been there before
Have you ever walked into an extremely dark room or been in a very dark place that provided absolutely no light? Or, have you been in a place that had the light on at one time, but suddenly the light turned off and you were left standing there, literally unable to see your hand in front of your face? I have . . . and it was a scary moment.

What a sight
I was with my daughter's school group as they took a tour through some mountain caverns. We entered the side of a mountain down through a long tunnel on a concrete walkway. With every downward step I quickly noticed that it was getting cooler and cooler in temperature. Then I noticed that the concrete walkway ended and I had begun to walk on dirt. Cold drips of water were dropping on my head as I walked every few steps along the path. The walkway began to narrow, causing some of the adults to have to duck down slightly in order to follow the tour guide deeper into the mountain's core. Everywhere I turned I saw beautiful crystalline drips, rounded flowstones, and huge stalactite and stalagmite formations (. . . impressed with my knowledge . . . who said you can't learn a lot on a third grade field trip!). Each scene was illuminated beautifully as a result of the strategically placed lighting. It was powerful enough to illuminate the beautiful formations while dim enough not to disturb the dozens of resting bats all along the cavern walls (Okay, beside the bats, I was beginning to really enjoy this!).

What did she just say?!
I remember the guide gathering us in front of one of these formations. She began to give us an update on how far we had traveled into the mountain and what the temperature was in this particular portion of the cavern. Then the guide informed us that she was going to do something in a moment that we were "not to get freaked-out about." "I am now going to turn off the lights," she said.

Grown men DO cry

Immediately, my heart began to pound 100xs a minute. And as I began to watch her walk over towards the circuit breaker I immediately got into my "providing/protecting" mode with my daughter. I instantly reached out and brought her close to me. I bent down to her ear and rapidly began giving her instructions—giving her no time to ask questions, debate, or deliberate upon. "You must not move!" "You must touch my hand at all times—do not let go." "No matter what you hear anyone else say, never leave my side." Then I increased my grip on her little shoulder probably to the point it was a bit uncomfortable for her. Then . . . CLICK—pure darkness.

I leaned down to where I had last seen my daughter's face, "Are you there?" I asked. "Yes, Daddy," she replied. "Are you okay?" I inquired. "Yep!" she replied. And after I knew she was okay and had not moved away, we began to talk to each other in the dark about how awesome it was to be experiencing this. "Whoa, it is so dark!" we echoed to each other. You could tell by the sound of our voices that we were now both smiling and enjoying the experience. A few seconds later, the lights came on and we all reflected on how we enjoyed those few moments.

Truth is your point of reference

In the same way, truth is that anchor—that "point of reference"—that we all should cling to in order to secure our bearings in life. And when there are many voices that may come calling to us to consider walking away from truth, we are to remain closely tethered to truth in order to navigate life's decisions.

> " IN THE SAME WAY, TRUTH IS THAT ANCHOR— THAT "POINT OF REFERENCE"—THAT WE ALL SHOULD CLING TO IN ORDER TO SECURE OUR BEARINGS IN LIFE. "

Truth is found in a person

Fortunately, truth is not found in a theory or concept—as they frequently change over time. According to the Bible, truth is found in a person—Jesus Christ. He reminded His disciples that, "I [Jesus] am the way, the truth, and the life. No one can come to the Father except through me" (John 14:6). And in knowing Him personally (see the chapter on "Salvation"), your life will experience true freedom: "And you will know the truth, and the truth will set you free" (John 8:32).

He is the one source of truth

Have you embraced the truth?

If you are a believer in Jesus Christ, cling very tightly and know He has embraced you very closely (John 10:27-30). Continue to submit to His authority, instructions and guidance, knowing that He always has the best in mind for your life (Philippians 4:6-7). If you have not yet placed your faith in Jesus Christ as your Savior, take a moment to consider what your point of reference is in your life. Is it your own feelings about things? Is your security contingent upon another person's confidence in their own view of life? Or, have you ever considered the question about truth? Take time to read on and consider the biblical truths that are highlighted in this book, and hopefully you will come to a more firm conclusion about Jesus Christ and your need for Him.

Study what the Bible says about the reality of truth
Here are some more verses to read on this topic—John 1:14, 14:6, 17:17, 18:38; Psalm 119:142,160; 1 John 5:6; 1 Timothy 2:7.

Write it down... →

...& make it HAPPEN!

SECTION TWO:

THE BIBLE

REVELATION

(REV-UH-LEY-SHU N)

> "Because humans are finite and God is infinite, if they are to know God it must come about by God's manifestation of himself. There are two basic classifications of revelation. General revelation is God's communication of himself to all persons at all times and in all places. Special revelation involves God's particular communications and manifestations of himself to particular persons at particular times, communications and manifestations that are available now only by consultation of certain sacred writings."
> - MILLARD ERICKSON, *Christian Theology,* 178

The Bible is a book of God's interaction with His creation. The first verse of the Bible starts not only with the assumption of a God (Genesis 1:1a, "In the beginning God"), but also with His creative work (Genesis 1:1b, "created the heavens and the earth"). The Bible indicates that God has revealed some things about Himself, but that He has not revealed everything there is to know about Him (Deuteronomy 29:29). In addition, the revelation of God has in a very real sense been progressive throughout the Bible. After the fall of mankind in Genesis 3, God has been progressively revealing more of Himself throughout the various generations of human history. Ultimately this revelation is most fully known in the person of Jesus Christ, who is God. So, the best picture we have of God is God Himself in human flesh, walking among us. We call this the incarnation (John 1:14 says, "So the Word became human and made his home among us").

There are two main categories of God's revelation. These two categories can be summarized as God's general revelation and God's special revelation. Psalm 19 presents us with a great picture of both of God's ways of revealing Himself. Psalm 19:1-6 speak of God's general revelation, as the psalmist recounts the splendor of God evidenced within God's creation. Verses 7-11 reflect on God's special revelation through recognition of God's Word to us.

It is important to keep in mind three things about God's revelation:

God's general revelation is available to everyone. The apostle Paul mentions the universality of God's general revelation in Romans 1. In this chapter Paul talks about the fact that even those far from God are without excuse since God's power is clearly seen through His works (verse 20).

General revelation is not enough to bring someone to salvation. Salvation itself is only a work of God, and we are told in John 14:6 and Acts 4:12 that salvation is only through Jesus. Paul also echoes this same thought in Romans 10. In this passage, the apostle Paul mentions that confession of Jesus Christ as Lord and belief in Jesus' resurrection are necessary for salvation. Paul is not arguing for an idea of works leading to salvation (as though salvation is earned), but rather, he is presenting an understanding that it takes a knowledge of these items for someone to be saved.

God took the initiative to reveal Himself to us. We did not discover God, as though He was hidden somewhere. This is an important point to keep in mind, because sometimes we present God as hiding Himself from us. In reality, He desires a relationship with us, and He has revealed much about Himself to us. Even in the Garden of Eden, right after Adam and Eve sinned by disobeying God, it was God who sought out Adam and Eve. They did not run from Him after they sinned, they hid from God.

PRACTICAL APPLICATION:

You've got to be joking?!

Have you ever encountered a person in your home town who made an astounding claim that they knew one of the most popular (and your favorite) actors in Hollywood? I can hear you now. Your jaw drops for a moment. You stare at them for a while. Then your voice raises an octave above your normal speaking voice as you exclaim, "No way?!" "You're joking with me." "You know him?!" "How do you know him?!" "Sure," your friend says. "We're really close. I know a lot about him! I know he prefers to eat at bistro's on Sundays, drives a black car, and he likes to use the word 'buddy' to his closest friends. He's not shy to stop and chat with you; he's got a great smile and a good sense of humor!"

Whoa! My friend must indeed know this actor! And in one millisecond, you began to dream up ways you yourself could take advantage of this newly discovered news. "Maybe I can get my friend here to connect me with the actor so that I can get his autograph!" "Maybe I can get a few pictures with the actor if my friend can hook me up with him!!" "Maybe my friend can hook us all up for lunch at some street-side café on Hollywood and Vine!!!" "Maybe we'll be seen by the paparazzi and a picture of all three of us can make the cover of a famous magazine!!!!" "Maybe he will like me . . . fall in love . . . get married . . . !!!!"

Then all of your dreams of grandeur are dashed and your excitement deflated when your friend explains how he truly "knows" this famous actor. "I actually shook his hand as he was walking from his limo to a restaurant . . . and he stopped and listened to me tell him that I was his greatest fan. He personally thanked me for my support and wished that every fan would be as loyal as I was to him. Then he patted me on the back, said 'thanks buddy'—yep, he called me his personal 'buddy'—and as he walked away, he made it a point to tell me to "take care." Did you hear that? He was that concerned about me that he expressed his care for me! Yep, I know him well."

There's a difference
After you withhold your anger and your desire to grab your hometown friend and shake him for an hour for foolishly getting your hopes up, you quickly understand that based upon what he told you, your hometown friend does not know that actor. You conclude that your friend is merely familiar with the actor, but he does not have a personal relationship with the actor. In fact, no matter how many times your friend captures the actor on a runway or sidewalk outside of a street-side bistro, he will never culti- vate an intimate relationship with the actor. At best, your home town friend will only become an expert at reciting basic knowledge that, frankly, any person could observe if they spent some time waiting outside a couple of restaurants themselves.

Love the general; embrace the special
Even though "general revelation" is unable to bring a person to the point of having their soul eternally changed, no believer in Jesus Christ should ig- nore the beauty of God's general revelation. General revelation still provides awesome opportunities to admire the grandiose power and majesty of God (i.e. mountains, landscape, atmosphere, universe, etc.). Even the Psalmist instructs all believers to adore the majestic creation of God that provides this general testimony of God's greatness. Psalm 19:1-4 says, "The heavens proclaim the glory of God. The skies display his craftsmanship. Day after day they continue to speak; night after night they make him known. They speak without a sound or word; their voice is never heard. Yet their mes- sage has gone throughout the earth, and their words to all the world."

> ❝ KNOWING THE DIFFERENCE BETWEEN THE TWO TYPES OF REVELATION WILL MAKE THE DIFFERENCE BETWEEN KNOWING ABOUT GOD AND PERSONALLY KNOWING GOD! ❞

Unlike general revelation that can only make someone "familiar" with the actions and power of God, special revelation is what is able to bring about true life-change to a human being. It is God's Word that we are instructed to know more and more each day. The prophet Jeremiah encouraged us to devour God's special Word in Jeremiah 15:16a, "When I discovered your words, I devoured them. They are my joy and my heart's delight."

The Psalmist also emphasized that it is this special revelation that is able to provide specific guidance in our lives, "I have hidden your word in my heart, that I might not sin against you" (Psalm119:11). Knowing the difference between the two types of revelation will make the difference between knowing about God and personally knowing God!

Study some more Bible verses that relate to general and special revelation

Here are some more verses to read on this topic—Psalm 19; Romans 1:18-21; Acts 14:15-17, 17:23-28; Psalm 119:105.

Don't agree w/ this comment? This is not salvation

Write it down... →

...& make it
HAPPEN!

INSPIRATION/INERRANCY

(IN-ER-UHN-SEE)

"We affirm that inspiration was the work in which God by His Spirit, through human writers, gave us His Word. The origin of Scripture is divine. The mode of divine inspiration remains largely a mystery to us . . . We deny that inspiration can be reduced to human insight, or to heightened states of consciousness of any kind."
- ARTICLE VII, CHICAGO STATEMENT OF BIBLICAL INERRANCY

The Bible is God-breathed according to 2 Timothy 3:16. The Greek term is theopneustos, and it means "inspired by God." The significance of this understanding is seen in the idea that the words of the Bible are not merely human words. The words that are in the Bible are the very words of God.

By inerrancy, we mean that the Bible does not contain any error. In a very real sense, the doctrine of inerrancy is an appeal to the very character of God. Since God is absolutely holy in His very being (Isaiah 6:3), that means His words would be absolutely holy as well. In addition, God's nature is all-knowing (omniscient), meaning that He would not err in His understanding. Because of the very nature of God, we can have confidence in the accuracy of His words to us. There are a few considerations that will be helpful to process through when considering the topics of inspiration and inerrancy.

First, it should be understood that the personality of the human author was incorporated into the pages of Scripture. God did not simply dictate the words of Scripture to the human authors, but rather, He used the giftedness and abilities of the writers of Scripture. This can be seen in the various writers and even in the terminology they use. Paul was a well-educated individual within the first century, and his writings reflect that educational level.

Second, the inspiration and inerrancy of the Bible point to its authority. If it is true that God is the authority, then that means that I am not the authority and you are not the authority. It means that you and I are accountable to Someone besides ourselves. For many that understanding brings with it great conviction, because they have been living their lives as though they are independent of God. For others, the idea of our accountability to God brings great comfort. They are able to rest in the assurance of God's provision. They are able to lay aside the burden they have been carrying for all the troubles of the world.

Finally, inspiration and inerrancy apply to the original manuscripts. Our modern-day translations are the Word of God only to the extent that they accurately reflect the original texts, which were produced under the inspiration of God. Without going into all of the details surrounding these statements, it is important to remember that the Bible is not what you or I acknowledge it to be. Rather, the Word of God is the Word of God. Period. Whether you or I like it or not, the Bible is the Word of God, and it is up to you and me to acknowledge this truth. We are to live our lives in light of the teachings God offers through the pages of the Bible. The writers of the Bible did not speak on their own initiative. As 2 Peter 1:21 states, the writers of Scripture spoke as they were "moved by the Holy Spirit." I believe God has preserved His Word and ensured that it has been reliably passed down from generation to generation.

PRACTICAL APPLICATION

A love-hate relationship

In my experience in ministerial practice, higher education, and familial contexts, "authority" seems to be a concept that people either love, hate, or flip-flop on, depending on the circumstance. In many contexts, some people prefer to blame or defer to authority when an unpleasant or unpopular decision has been made so as to distance themselves from any culpability and responsibility for the decision. Then, the same people turn around and appreciate the cover of protection that leadership provides employees, family members, and parishioners. It seems that authority is beloved when it assists us in what we want to accomplish, and it is a hindrance to us achieving our goals when it dictates what we can and cannot do. So, what is our proper attitude towards "authority."

It comes down to trust

Authority is readily accepted by another when there is strong trust in the leader. Where trust has been demonstrated and proven to be reliable, people will be happy to accept the authority of a leader. And once the leader holds the trust card with someone, he/she is able to offer guidance, directives, and prescriptions that are accepted swiftly. Loyalty is virtually certain. If there is no trust, then people will not receive the directives from the authority with loyal hearts. At best, the leader will get "compliance" but not loyalty. But most of the time the people will attempt to bypass the directive, ignore the leader's instruction, and downplay the urgency stressed by the leader. It all comes down to proven trust.

Trust God—trust His Word

The Bible is God's delivered "Word" to every human being. It is full of portraits of His beautiful creation of every person, His unconditional love, His invitation for all to receive His mercy and forgiveness of sins (see the chapter on "Salvation"), and His ultimate plan for all human beings who have ever lived upon the earth. It provides both general and specific direction for our lives so that we will not experience spiritual devastation by making

38

poor choices (see the chapter on "Canon"). It is the solely sufficient source of truth that God has placed in our possession to guide us for living today.

An unfortunate observation
The following should be read in the spirit in which we wish these next few statements to be received—in the most sincere, respectful manner possible as a way to broach a portion of the "authority" question that does not get addressed too often in biblical writings. I have found that however some-one views the Bible—"a bunch of do's and don'ts" . . . "a great guide-book for life" . . . "unnecessary to live an 'ok' life" . . . "not correct 100% of the time" . . . etc., I have learned one thing to be true 100 percent of the time—pride will keep a soul from accepting God's authority. With all due respect, it has become easier and easier to observe this in peoples' lives the more we interact with even the most sincere "seekers" of religion and truth. Ulti-mately, every discussion that we have engaged in regarding God and truth has come down to someone does not accept God's authority in their lives. Which, even in the most respectful of persons it comes down to the root of pride (i.e., not desiring to have God's authority over their own authority). Whether this pride is packaged in a violent, aggressive way towards God or whether it is touted as a result of calm, thoughtful deduction, the root is the same. So, while we relish any and all opportunities to discuss spiritual truth with anyone (truly!)—even in the most respectful of discussions, the question of who is going to be the authority over one's life always comes up.

> " I HAVE LEARNED ONE THING TO BE TRUE 100 PERCENT OF THE TIME—PRIDE WILL KEEP A SOUL FROM ACCEPTING GOD'S AUTHORITY. "

Are you searching?
Admittedly, there are some people who say, "By no means do I want to be disrespectful to God and the Bible—absolutely not! I am just taking my time to determine if God and the Bible are trustworthy." And I totally understand what the person is saying. They are respectable, sincere, and not being hostile in any way—just searching for the truth. These discussions are often constructive and pleasant, and I appreciate this spirit very much. But ultimately, every person has to determine if they will ever allow their hearts to submit to God's authority to the point of saying, "I will submit to You in all things in my life." Our hope is that this moment comes swiftly in peoples' lives because of the sobering reality that, "How do you know what your life will be like tomorrow? Your life is like the morning fog—it's here a little while, then it's gone" (James 4:14). And, unfortunately, in my experi-ence, I have seen more times than not that if a seeker takes too much time

"searching," their heart will gravitate towards a self-adjudicating philosophy of life rather than feeling compelled to submit to God's authority (c.f. "You must warn each other every day, while it is still 'today,' so that none of you will be deceived by sin and hardened against God," Hebrews 3:13).

Talk it out
Take time to talk with someone who is a believer in Jesus Christ about the "authority" question. Ask him/her to be honest. Ask them to join in your spiritual journey. And if you have settled the authority question in your mind and have submitted to God's authority through His Word, then seek someone out to partner with in order to share your experiences, questions, and your ultimate decision to accept His authority over your life. Regard-less of which side of this equation you are on, sharing your heart can only sharpen each other spiritually—"As iron sharpens iron, so a friend sharpens a friend" (Proverbs 27:17).

Study what the Bible says about inspiration and inerrancy
Here are some more verses to read on this topic —2 Timothy 3:16; 2Peter 1:20-21; Acts 1:16; Hebrews 3:7.

Write it down... ↘

...& make it
HAPPEN!

PRAXIS

INTERPRETATION

(IN-TUR-PRI-TEY-SHUHN)

"**Hermeneutics**. The discipline that studies the principles and theories of how texts ought to be interpreted, particularly sacred texts such as the Scriptures. Hermeneutics also concerns itself with understanding the unique roles and relationships between the author, the text and the original or subsequent readers."
- POCKET DICTIONARY OF THEOLOGICAL TERMS, 59

I can still remember the words of my Old Testament university professor. He would often say, "The Bible can never mean what it never meant." There is a great and intimidating burden placed on the individual who studies the Bible to make sure he or she is going through the necessary steps to accurately understand what God is revealing about Himself in the pages of the text. Even in Jesus' own ministry on earth, He acknowledged that it was necessary to study and interpret the Scripture of His day. John 5:39 states, "You search the Scriptures because you think they give you eternal life. But the Scriptures point to me!" He is challenging His audience to recognize Him through the Old Testament.

It is important that we take the interpretation of God's Word seriously. Too often we try to make the Bible something that the original author never intended the Bible to say, or something that the original audience never understood from the text. Many times this is not intentional. It is an innocent misunderstanding of the original context of the passage of Scripture, and it is a reflection of processing what we read through our own experience. There is an entire field of study dedicated to the correct interpretation of the Bible. This field is known as hermeneutics.

The three basic steps to understanding the Bible are (1) observation, (2) interpretation and (3) application. By following these steps, students of the Bible can be more confident in their understanding of the Bible.

The first step is **observation**. I think we have all been guilty of reading a verse of Scripture and immediately asking, "how does this apply to me," or "what does this verse mean to me." The problem with this method is that we can quickly come to the wrong conclusion about a passage of the Bible. We can easily understand the Bible to be saying something that God never intended to communicate. A better practice is to start with a simple observation of what is being said in the text itself through a basic understanding of the historical context of the passage. For instance, it would be important to know that the apostle Paul was highly educated and trained in the legal issues of his Jewish society. Many of his writings were written like a courtroom brief, which reflects his training and giftedness. Knowing some information about Paul can help you to interpret his writings.

The second step in the process of understanding the Word of God is **interpretation**. It is at this point that we seek to understand what exactly is being communicated about God in the passage. Paul encourages Timothy in 2 Timothy 2:15 to, "Work hard so you can present yourself to God and receive his approval. Be a good worker, one who does not need to be ashamed and who correctly explains the word of truth." The idea of "correctly explains" in the Greek language is the word, orthotome , which means to handle correctly or to "cut straight." Paul desires that Timothy accurately and correctly handle the Word of God.

Finally, the interpretation of the passage should be related to your life in a personal way. The third step in understanding the Bible is the process of **application**. Many times I have found that when I take the extra time to really do my research on a particular passage, the meaning and application of the material is much more powerful than if I just try to jump to the application of the text. The Bible is a book which is ultimately about God, but it is also a book that tells us a lot about ourselves. It is a book that has great application to our lives on a daily basis, but it is important that you and I diligently study the Scripture, so that we live our lives based on the foundation of the Word of God.

PRACTICAL APPLICATION:

A nice gift
God delivered His Holy Word to mankind in familiar languages of that era and in that particular culture. This is a huge benefit to anyone who desires to study God's messages to us. In delivering His Holy Word in this fashion, we are actually able to study His Word intelligently. From history we know the societies, cultural practices, grammatical idioms, word origins, social customs, and specific languages of the societies from which God's Holy Word was written (i.e., The New Testament was written in Koine Greek, and the Old Testament was written in Hebrew and Aramaic). God made it very easy for finite human beings to do something otherwise impossible—study His Word in known dialects.

" GOD MADE IT VERY EASY FOR FINITE HUMAN BEINGS TO DO SOMETHING OTHERWISE IMPOSSIBLE—STUDY HIS WORD IN KNOWN DIALECTS."

No PhD required

Fortunately, you do not have to be an expert linguist to know what God's life-changing messages mean to you. The Bible is crystal clear as to its essential teachings. You can experience personal salvation (see the chapter on "Salvation"), mature spiritually as a believer in Jesus Christ and experience intimacy with God by simply reading the Bible . . . in your own language . . . without any study/reference tools at your disposal. This should be encouraging to those who are not inclined to collegiate-level study and deep historical/cultural research. But for those who desire to pursue a more detailed study of the Bible, the exercise will not disappoint.

Stand in their sandals

When interpreting the written words of the Bible, it is always wise to focus on determining how the listener of that day received the teaching. If you don't do this step, you will fall into the common trap of connecting a twenty-first century application with a first century phrase or occurrence. This creates a scenario that never could have possibly happened. For example, what do you think when you read these words of Jesus, "The Father and I are one"? Does He mean that the Father and Jesus are simply one-in-purpose, or unified in their message, or is it an actual claim by Jesus to be God? The best way to interpret that phrase is to ask, "How did the people listening to these words first-hand interpret them?" Answer: They accepted it as a claim by Jesus to be God Himself. How do we know that? John 10:31-33 actually is provided in order to assist us—the twenty-first century reader—in interpreting the statement. "Once again the people picked up stones to kill him. Jesus said, " 'At my Father's direction I have done many good works. For which one are you going to stone me?' They replied, 'We're stoning you not for any good work, but for blasphemy! You, a mere man, claim to be God.' "

But sometimes there is not this clear of an interpretive solution. In these instances, you can start by researching the cultural elements of the day. Often that gives clarity to the text in question. You can also research all of the crystal clear verses in the Bible that address the same subject matter that you are trying to interpret. There are online Bible Concordances that list verses by topic, so this research tool is readily available. When you compare multiple verses that speak to the same subject, the result will be a more accurate interpretation of the passage in question. There are more Bible study tools listed below.

Not an impossible task

There are some good reference tools to assist any student of the Bible in better understanding the context and culture of the Bible. There is not enough room in this chapter to list all of the helpful resources to assist you in your further study of the culture of the biblical writings, but my good friends at Broadman and Holman Publishing Group provide numerous books that deal with biblical commentaries, manners and customs, Bible backgrounds, and surveys of the Old and New Testaments. Ultimately, the Holy Spirit will guide any believer in Jesus Christ in the study of the Holy Bible. And in those times where the meaning remains unclear, He will teach you how to retain your God-honoring testimony as you charitably interact with each other in your discussions about the Bible . " . . . the Holy Spirit— he will teach you everything and will remind you of everything I have told you" (John 14:26b). "When the Spirit of truth comes, he will guide you into all truth . . ." (John 16:13a).

Study what the Bible says about the importance of accurately interpreting the Bible
Here are some more verses to read on this topic—2 Timothy 2:15; Luke 24:25-27; Acts 17:11; Mark 12:24.

Write it down...↘

...& make it
HAPPEN!

ILLUMINATION

(IH-LOO-MUH-NEY-SHUHN)

"In relation to the Bible, the doctrine of revelation relates to the unveiling of truth in the material of the Scriptures; inspiration concerns the method by which the Holy Spirit superintended the writing of Scripture; and illumination refers to the ministry of the Spirit by which the meaning of Scripture is made clear to the believer."
- EVANGELICAL DICTIONARY OF THEOLOGY, 590-591

John 14 speaks of the ministry of the Holy Spirit as being an "Advocate" or a "Helper" (verses 16 and 26). As part of this help, God's Word tells us that the Holy Spirit "will teach you everything and will remind you of everything I have told you" (v. 26). It is this ministry of the Holy Spirit where He comes alongside the believer to shed light on the biblical message, which is being referred to in the teachings on the ministry of illumination.

Within the ministry of illumination there is a sense in which the Holy Spirit removes the veil of spiritual blindness that characterizes the unbelieving individual (2 Corinthians 4:4). With the removal of the veil, the Holy Spirit is then able to allow the truth of God's Word to speak to the person. In a positive sense, the Holy Spirit is shedding light on the inspired Word of God.

The Holy Spirit's ministry of illumination assists us in our ongoing study of the Bible to discover the correct interpretation. The Holy Spirit is always working with the individual to reveal the truth of God's Word. A good example of the working of the Holy Spirit (as well as diligent study on the part of the individual) is seen in Acts 17:10-15, where the apostle Paul's interaction with the believers at Berea is recorded. As Paul taught the people at Berea, verse 11 says that "They searched the Scriptures day after day to see if Paul and Silas were teaching the truth." This is a great example of a community of believers taking the initiative to study the Word of God, not taking for granted the assistance of the Holy Spirit in their lives. Personal study and the work of the Holy Spirit operate together toward the end result of correct interpretation.

Keep in mind also that the work of the Holy Spirit in illuminating the Scriptures is an ongoing process. It is understood that a person will need to read a passage of Scripture more than once in order to fully understand its meaning. There is great significance to the idea of the progressive nature of God's revelation throughout the history of His working with mankind, and also the individual stages at which we progress as we draw closer to Jesus.

Through the work of the Holy Spirit, we can better prepare ourselves for serving Jesus, but we should not expect to know everything about Jesus the first time we hear a passage of Scripture read.

PRACTICAL APPLICATION:

Would somebody turn on a light?

I recently took my good friend through a haunted house. And though I would consider him to be a strong and confident person, something happened when he entered the haunted house. This strong, professionally accomplished man shuddered like a scared child. (BTW—If you ever want to know which of your closest friends would courageously help you in the midst of dire circumstances, just test them out by taking them through a haunted house! You'll quickly see who would be your courageous protector and who would cower under even the least scary circumstances.)

When we were half way through the haunted house—in the belly of this huge mansion—we entered the all-too-familiar maze of narrow black-painted walls that forced us to navigate in complete and utter darkness. Immediately, I reached out to my friend who was walking in front of me in order to hold on to his sweatshirt as I followed him through the maze. To my surprise, he navigated it pretty well. Then, all of a sudden, I heard a "THUD" as he ran into one of the side walls of the maze. He then stopped completely—causing everyone in the line behind us to collide and ultimately slam into my back. Admittedly, it started to get a bit crowded and a little scary not knowing where we were, where we should be going and who was in front or behind us.

People began to shout, "Hey!" "What's going on up there?" "Someone turn on a light!" Hearing their words, my friend reached into his pocket, grabbed his cell phone, and turned on the brightest light his phone could generate. Then he continued to walk. His son turned to him and said, "Dad, turn off the light! That isn't cool! You're not supposed to do that!" "But I can't see and this helps," he replied. Immediately I thought to myself, "Well, I don't like to admit it, but I too like his cell phone light. Now, I can see everything that's going to jump out at me!" For the rest of our time in the haunted house, I never attempted to get him to put his phone away.

You will not be left in the dark

Jesus told His closest friends that after He died, physically rose again from the dead and ascended back to heaven, He would make sure that they had another equally powerful guide who would remind them of Jesus' teachings. And this guide would also lead them to know how to apply biblical truths in every unique situation that would come into their lives. Jesus was referring to God the Holy Spirit. John 14:26-27 captures this dialogue between Jesus and His close friends, "But when the Father sends the

Advocate as my representative—that is, the Holy Spirit—he will teach you everything and will remind you of everything I have told you. I am leaving you with a gift—peace of mind and heart. And the peace I give is a gift the world cannot give. So don't be troubled or afraid."

Listen to the Light Bearer
The Holy Spirit is the guide by which all believers find clarity and direction in their lives. The Holy Spirit assists us in understanding what the Holy Scriptures mean. He also convicts us when we are living contrary to the will of God for our lives, and He produces a kindred fellowship among other believers. And just like I placed my hand upon the shoulder of my friend while in the middle of darkness, we too should strive to remain very close to the Holy Spirit through the reading of God's Word and personal prayer. As He brings conviction, be quick to confess your sin and disobedience, so you don't grieve the Holy Spirit in His attempt to guide you. Disobedience has the potential to muffle the Holy Spirit's message to your heart.

" THE HOLY SPIRIT IS THE GUIDE BY WHICH ALL BELIEVERS FIND CLARITY AND DIRECTION IN THEIR LIVES. "

One step at a time
And while the Holy Spirit is the One with whom we receive spiritual guidance in our lives, we ought not to get frustrated when God provides us with just enough light to negotiate only one turn at a time in the dark maze of life. Don't expect or assume that God will illuminate the entire path for you in one moment. What He does promise to do is to provide each of us with enough illumination to keep us on the right path. Try not to run in front of Him. And don't lag behind Him. Walk close behind Him and trust the pace and the path where He leads you.

Study some more Bible verses that relate to the Holy Spirit providing illumination
Here are some more verses to read on this topic—John 14; 1 Corinthians 2:12; Luke 24:27,44-48.

Write it down... ↘

...& make it
HAPPEN!

CANON

(KAN-UHN)

"The word "canon" (Greek. for "a rule") is applied to the Bible in two ways: first, in regard to the Bible as the church's standard of faith and practice, and second, in regard to its contents as the correct collection and list of inspired books."
- ESV STUDY BIBLE, "The Canon of Scripture," 2577

The word canon itself is a Greek term meaning "measuring rod" or "standard." It is not a word that is found in the Bible, but even within the pages of Scripture there is the recognition of sacred books. Most conversations involving the canon of Scripture revolve around the twenty-seven books of the New Testament. Throughout His ministry, Jesus spoke to the authority of the Old Testament. For instance, He mentions the "the law of Moses and the prophets and in the Psalms" in Luke 24:44-48. We will primarily focus our attention on the New Testament books as well.

There are questions as to how the standard, the Canon, of the twenty-seven books of the New Testament was established. Most individuals are surprised to hear that the first recorded mention of a list of the twenty-seven books of the New Testament was in a letter written by Athanasius in 367 AD. A few years later two church councils (Council of Hippo in 393 and Council of Carthage in 397) presented the twenty-seven books that comprise the Christian Bible's New Testament. This caused some to fear that for nearly 350 years the earlier church did not know what was to be considered Scripture, or that somehow the council voted to make certain books authoritative. However, that fear is very far from the truth.

In reality, the early establishment of the canon of the New Testament is well documented as being very close to the actual writing of the books in the first century AD. Consider that the apostle Peter calls the writings of Paul "Scripture" in 2 Peter 3:15-16. Also passages like 1Thessalonians 2:13 and 1 Peter 1:10-12 acknowledge the canonicity of the writings of Scripture. In addition to the apostles themselves, the early church leaders recognized the writings as being from God. Three of the most prominent early church fathers who lived within a generation of the death of the disciples are Clement of Rome, Ignatius, and Polycarp. Included within their writings are numerous references to the Scriptures of the New Testament.

We have to remember that the first few centuries of the early church were much different times than what we experience today. We are told concerning the birth of Jesus that, "when the right time came, God sent his Son, born of a woman, subject to the law" (Galatians 4:4-5). I believe a similar statement could be said of the timeline related to the New Testament canon. The timing of the third and fourth centuries was right for the official recognition of the canon of the New Testament. That does not mean that those prior to 393 AD did not have the Bible, but rather with the rise of false beliefs, false teachings and the increase in false books (claiming to be Scripture), it was appropriate at that time to officially recognize the authority which these twenty-seven books already possessed.

PRACTICAL APPLICATION:

Keep it on the road

Surrounding Liberty University in Central Virginia are the beautiful Blue Ridge Mountains. There is nothing like them in the late autumn months when all the trees begin to change color. Everywhere you look are beautiful shades of red, orange, yellow, and burgundy. And the beautiful landscape goes for hundreds of miles. It is truly captivating. This is the favorite season for all of the convertible-owners along with the motorcyclists in the area. From morning to night, motorcyclists, leisure drivers, along with cyclists, hikers and joggers all venture outside to take in this breathtaking gift from God.

When the night falls and the crowds begin to disperse and return home, the same mountains that once provided a beautiful view of God's creation now seem to trap the traveler in highly-elevated, extremely steep roads that twist and turn sharply. And with no street lights to assist in the journey, these 15 mph max turns can be very unnerving—especially knowing that on one side of the road is a cliff that could potentially drop off over 100 feet. And as the cool mist of the mountain air begins to fog a warm windshield, the fear of falling off a cliff increases. Fortunately, the traveler is not without protection.

Along every stretch of the mountain road are miles of protective guardrails. They line every inch of the road that borders a dangerous cliff and most of the opposite side of the road if there is a concern about falling rock. And while these guardrails will certainly do a number on your vehicle if you strike them from any direction, they will certainly save your life from certain death from either falling off the cliff or running into a stray boulder or two.

These protective guardrails are not tourist attractions. No one buys a new convertible in order to drop the top down and cruise the Blue Ridge Parkway so they can get an unobstructed view of the guardrails. These rusty, old protectors tend not to be the center of discussion when the Sunday drivers are cruising around on a leisurely day. But they quickly become the center of discussion when they protect someone's car from launching over the cliff. And at that moment, people begin to appreciate the leader ship who put those protective parameters into place. People are grateful to those who had the wisdom to place the guardrails there to save lives. Sometimes, people actually feel compelled to write letters and make phone calls to the community leadership who had the foresight to put these protective guards on the roads.

Check out the beautiful guardrail

The Bible is God's protective guardrail that has been formulated and placed as a defined boundary in which and with which every human being must function. While the Bible has many purposes—"All Scripture is inspired by God and is useful to teach us what is true and to make us realize what is wrong in our lives. It corrects us when we are wrong and teaches us to do what is right. God uses it to prepare and equip his people to do every good work" (2 Tim. 3:16-17). The Bible was written and completed in order to keep us from falling off of the proverbial cliff. And while it does not get the attention it ought to in today's society, God's Word actually supersedes any other authority—both written and spoken—by any human being in today's world. It is the Old and New Testaments of the Holy Bible that provide the parameters by which every person should live. And while some people bristle at being given parameters in life, the wise person chooses not to ignore God's parameters. The wise person fights the tendency to be repulsed by God's guardrails. And the wise person actually sees God's clear guidance and truth contained in the Holy Bible as life-saving, protective spiritual guardrails that align one's journey in life.

> **" THE BIBLE WAS WRITTEN AND COMPLETED IN ORDER TO KEEP US FROM FALLING OFF OF THE PROVERBIAL CLIFF. "**

This week, why don't you consider these thoughts based upon our discussion regarding God's Word:

1. Take a walk

Literally, take a walk amid God's creation. In Virginia, many people who believe this reality about the Holy Bible find themselves taking their Bibles with them when they cruise along the Blue Ridge mountains. They stop somewhere along the way to read it and be reminded of the Creator of the beautiful mountains and the Protector of all who call Him "Lord" (cf. Psalm 121). Likewise, take a Bible with you and pause a few moments from your busy hectic life. Take time to thank God for His beautiful creation and for the truth that you hold in your hand.

2. Meditate upon God's Word

It is one thing to visually see God's artistic work in His creation (see the chapter on "Revelation"), but it is a totally different thing to receive God's direct instructions to you—His direct words to you—from the Holy Bible. Take time to read a portion of the Bible today. But don't just read it—meditate upon it. Ponder it. Discuss it with people within your church family (see the chapter on "church membership" and "ecclesia" (church). If you do this application, God's truth will become more than an academic and conceptual exercise, you will begin to experience the truths of the Bible.

3. Trust the only authoritative source of God's Holy Word — the Holy Bible

The Bible is the only authoritative source of God's Holy Word—The Holy Bible (the Old and New Testaments). There is no parallel. The Bible is not one of many authoritative written sources of truth. It is the only authoritative, sufficient source of the inspired Word of God. Therefore, take confidence in its teachings. As you read every word, you are hearing directly from God, the Creator of the universe who wants to have a personal relationship with you.

Study what the Bible says about the Word of God, its purpose, and the role of truth in a believer's life.
Here are some more verses to read on this topic— Luke 24:44-48; Hebrews 1:1-4; 2 Peter 3:15-16; 1 Thessalonians 2:13; 1 Peter 1:10-12.

Write it down... ↘

...& make it
HAPPEN!

SECTION THREE:
MANKIND/SIN

IMAGE OF GOD

(IM-IJ)

#1

"The image is something in the very nature of humans, in the way
they were made. It refers to something a human is rather than
something a human has or does. By virtue of being human, one
is in the image of God; it is not dependent upon the presence of
anything else."
- MILLARD ERICKSON, *Christian Theology*, 532

"Then God said, 'Let us make human beings in our image, to be like us.
They will reign over the fish in the sea, the birds in the sky, the livestock, all
the wild animals on the earth, and the small animals that scurry along the
ground.'" I believe that the concept of the image of God is one of the most
misunderstood doctrines in the Bible. I find this misunderstanding to be
very discouraging, since the doctrine should tell people something about
their Creator and something about oneself. However, I am encouraged by
the thought that clarification concerning this doctrine can help us to better
understand each other. And it can also better help us honor God with our
lives.

The Hebrew word for "image" is tselem (tseh'·lem), and it is often translated outside of Genesis 1:26-27 as something that is a physical representation. This provides us with a possible understanding of being created in
God's image. Theologians have identified possible interpretations of the
image of God, which range from mankind's ability to reign over the rest
of God's creation to the interpersonal relationships that we are able to
enter into with each other. Although there are many possibilities, it seems
likely from studying the context of the writing of Genesis that the author
(Moses) was explaining to his audience that mankind is created in order to
represent God here on earth. Similar to the way in which a conquering king
would erect a statue of himself in a foreign land, so that the people of the
country would know who they serve. Being created in the image of God
should help to point one another to the King of Kings. *#2*

How sad it is to think of the terrible damage which was done by mankind's
sin. Instead of looking to one another and pointing to God as our King, we
now make gods out of each other, we fight with one another, and we lie
and steal from one another. *#3*

King David reflected on the uniqueness of being created in God's image,
and he proclaimed praise to God for this wonderful creation. In Psalm 139
he states, "Thank you for making me so wonderfully complex! Your work-

manship is marvelous—how well I know it."

⊬3

The image of God is also spoken of in the New Testament. Jesus is said to perfectly represent God the Father. We know this from Jesus' own words in John 10:30 and John 14:1-14. Also, the apostle Paul talks about Jesus in Colossians 1:15-20. In verse 15 Paul says, "Christ is the visible image of the invisible God." Christians are said to be made into the image of Christ. Romans 8:29 tells us that those who have faith in Jesus are in an ongoing process of being made into the likeness of Jesus. We become more and more like Jesus as we surrender our lives to Him.

PRACTICAL APPLICATION:

You are amazing

Human beings are the most fantastic creations out of all of God's creative designs. Though there are some pretty extraordinary things that other creations of God can do, it is hard to rival the full capacity of creativity, uniqueness and knowledge of human beings. The problem is that because of mankind's choice to sin, all of mankind is tainted (see the chapter on "Sin"). We only are able to display a skewed, polluted image of our Creator. And because of this stain of sin upon every human heart, we are able to be easily swayed by our own fallen reasoning to ignore God and believe we are able to be the final authority in our lives. Fortunately, we have the Bible which is God's source from which to glean God's truth about ourselves. It is our foundation of instruction for how we should view our lives along with our need for God to guide us each day.

Love the gift and the Giver

One of the ways that we forget our fallen spiritual state is when we begin to focus on God's marvelous creation and forget to focus on the Creator. This is where mankind marvels at, say, the seemingly mesmerizing effect of music. Some of us begin to focus entirely on experiencing its effects—to the point that we will run to music to find peace, joy, and contentment in our lives. To some this may sound a bit extreme and unrealistic, but if you have ever engaged a serious musician who is earnest in pursuing the art, then you know that this scenario has great potential to draw a musical artist's full attention. Don't get me wrong, there is no problem with deeply loving music. Not at all. But when the focus is solely on God's beautiful creation, there is the potential to end up worshiping the creation with our thoughts and actions. Unfortunately, some even become dependent upon it. And this can occur with almost everything— music, work, hiking, nature, etc.

The Bible explains the beauty of the world and the purpose of all life, and it turns our focus upon the Author and Creator of all that we enjoy in this world. But just as we can be overtaken by the beauty of creation, the Bible reminds us that we should never forget to worship the Creator of the creation. Romans 1:25 cautions us that this tendency is due to the sin that has affected our hearts and lives:

"They traded the truth about God for a lie. So they worshiped and served the things God created instead of the Creator himself, who is worthy of eternal praise"(Romans 1:25)!

Fortunately, human beings are not without hope to gain the correct spiritual focus on our lives that we ought to have.

What's your status?
We are all creations of God, but we are not all His children. There is a big difference. In this book we share biblical details on how a person can accept Jesus Christ as his/her personal Savior (see the chapter on "Salvation"), but at this point it is important to note that man can never truly experience the full value of God's gifts in this world without first understanding your current relationship to God. It will not be perfect until you confess to Him through repentance for the sin in your life, accept Jesus Christ's sufficient payment for your sin, and commit to become dependent upon Him, the Creator of the world, to grant you salvation. With salvation comes a proper perspective on the world, creation and your beautiful role in it all.

> ❝ WITH SALVATION COMES A PROPER PERSPEC-
> TIVE ON THE WORLD, CREATION AND YOUR
> BEAUTIFUL ROLE IN IT ALL. ❞

Study what the Bible says about how mankind is created in the image of God
Here are some more verses to read on this topic—Genesis 1:26-27, 5:1, 9:6; James 3:9; Psalm 8, 139:13-16; Colossians 1:15-23.

Write it down... ⟿

...& make it
HAPPEN!

SIN

(SIN)

"Sin is any evil action or evil motive that is in opposition to God.
Simply put, sin is failure to let God be God and placing something
or someone in God's rightful place of supremacy."
- MILLARD ERICKSON, *Christian Theology*, 579

You and I call sin many different things. We may call it, "addiction," or perhaps, "impulse." Society calls disobedience by many different terms, but the Bible calls disobedience to the commands of God, sin. Sin is recognized within the Bible as the main problem with which you and I deal. It has many faces. We are born sinful (Psalm 51:5) and we are slaves to sin (Romans 6:1-14). We are also told that sin eventually leads to death (Romans 6:23). The first sin is recorded in the Bible in Genesis 3. The context of the story relates to a command that God gave Adam and Eve to not eat of the tree of the knowledge of good and evil. Entering into this story is Satan, the deceiver. We see in Genesis 3:1 that Satan starts to question Eve about the command of God. Satan challenges the very words of God, and by doing so, Satan is attacking the very character of God. He is deceiving Eve into believing that God really isn't good. The rest of Genesis 3 recounts the story, and the rest of the Bible is the story of God's redeeming love to overcome mankind's sin.

But what exactly is sin? Is it a sin to think a bad thought? Is it a sin to be tempted? The Bible says that Jesus was tempted (Matthew 4), and yet the Bible also says that Jesus was without sin (Hebrews 4:15). There are many words in the New Testament that talk about sin (actually six different Greek words). These words include the ideas of missing the mark, trespassing against someone else, doing something that is wicked, and failing to perform an obligation. The most popular is the word, hamartia, which means to "miss the mark." Picture an archer shooting at a target. To miss the bulls eye is to miss the mark. The Bible lets us know that this can be in an action that we do (or fail to do), and it can also be in our words, or our intentions.

After King David sinned a terrible sin (by committing adultery and murder), he prayed the following prayer, "You do not desire a sacrifice, or I would offer one. You do not want a burnt offering. The sacrifice you desire is a broken spirit. You will not reject a broken and repentant heart, O God." (Psalm 51:16-17) These verses are not meant to indicate that God does not desire sacrifices (verse 19 acknowledges that true sacrifices would be accepted). If you remember the Old Testament, you know the significance of the sacrifices of animals for a covering of sin. The point David is acknowledging is that God does not want something (in this case a sacrifice) if it is done with the wrong attitude (or heart condition).

What God desires, what He commands of His followers, is for us to let Him be God. This means that you and I need to obey God, and take Him at His word. We see that Satan knows God's Word, and that Satan tried to deceive us by twisting God's Word. Even when Satan tempted Jesus in the wilderness, he twisted God's Word to try to get Jesus to sin (Matthew 4). This means that you and I need to know God's Word and trust in Jesus' commands.

PRACTICAL APPLICATION:

No exceptions
Sin has affected all of our lives—every human being. Some people have acted upon their sin in horrific and grotesque ways while some have demonstrated the reality of sin in their lives in seemingly "non-offensive" ways (i.e., little white lies, stealing only little trinkets, etc.). And while society will be quick to accept the latter person and still conclude that the person is a law-abiding citizen, in God's eyes both offenders listed above have sin in their hearts.

> " SIN HAS AFFECTED ALL OF OUR LIVES—EVERY HUMAN BEING. "

Of course, people who are "law-abiding" citizens do not appreciate being placed in the same category with someone who has committed grievous offenses. "There must be a difference between the two," some have said. There must be since civil laws punish someone differently for committing a heinous crime versus someone who steals a clump of grapes in a grocery store and eats them while they shop without paying for them, right?

So, is there a difference between these two people?

Back to kindergarten
While the repercussions of someone's actions can/should indeed be different, the same sin nature is active in both of the individuals. And though some people exhibit their sinfulness in more overt ways than others, the same sin nature is alive and well in every person's life.

The best way I can describe how every person has the same sin nature, but each displays sinful actions differently is in the following illustration. On a scratch piece of paper (possibly in the margin of this page), I want you to take a pen and draw a circle. Then, I want you to think back to Kindergarten and how you used to draw a sun shining in the sky. Remember how you put stick lines coming out from the sun that would represent the rays of the sun? Some lines were long, some were short. Do the same with the circle you have just drawn. Draw a sun with stick lines coming out from it, representing the rays that come out of the sun. Now, let me explain how this describes the difference between a person's sinfulness/sinful nature and their sinful actions.

Imagine for a moment that the circle represents your sinful nature (i.e., your heart that has been tainted by sin—(see the chapter on the "Image of God"). It is true of every human being and each of us is culpable (i.e., responsible) for our sinful nature. Now imagine that the rays that you drew represent the sinful actions that you commit that obviously are produced by your sinful nature. This illustrates that the sinful nature is equally present in every person's life, but the amount of sinful acts can vary from person to person. Some people will exhibit more sinful actions and some people will exhibit fewer acts of sin—we will all act out our sinfulness in different ways BUT we all sin out of the same sinful nature!

How "sinful" are you?
I wonder how many rays of the sun you drew in your drawing—10 rays?—15 rays?—20 rays or more? In fact, I wonder if you did this exercise with someone else, how many rays you would have drawn compared to the amount of rays your friend would have drawn. I suspect that each of your number of rays would be different. In fact, I just did this exercise, and I drew eight rays (four long rays and four short rays). You might have drawn fewer rays than me. Though, if you were in the mood to doodle, you might have really engaged in this assignment, resulting in a lot of rays coming from the sun. So, how many did you draw?

The point is, some people exhibit more sinful actions than others—and yes, in today's society, they will receive more discipline for their excessive actions. But in God's eyes, every single person has an equally sinful nature that must be forgiven and cleaned up. No exceptions. Therefore, in order to have peace with God and be in good standing with Him, you must deal with your sinful nature (see the chapter on "Salvation"). Simply comparing your low amount of sinful acts to other people's high amounts does not mean that you can claim that you are better than most others.

Help!
What can you do to wash yourself of your sinful nature? Nothing. While you could certainly change the rays of the sun (by doing good things, going to a support group, changing your actions, etc.), you are unable to clean up your sinful nature that is resident in your heart. It is impossible. Only God can touch that part of your soul—not you. So, you need God to forgive you

HEART

(HAHRT)

#3

"The 'heart' stands for the inner being of man, the man himself.
As such, it is the fountain of all he does (Proverbs 4:4). All his
thoughts, desires, words, and actions flow from deep within him.
Yet a man cannot understand his own 'heart' (Jeremiah 17:9). As
a man goes on in his own way, his 'heart' becomes harder and
harder. But God will circumcise (cut away the uncleanness of) the
'heart' of His people, so that they will love and obey Him with their
whole being (Deuteronomy 30:6)."
- VINE'S COMPLETE EXPOSITORY DICTIONARY OF
THE OLD AND NEW TESTAMENTS, 109

We are told in Matthew 22:37, "You must love the LORD your God with all
your heart, all your soul, and all your mind." We ask children if they have
asked Jesus into their hearts. The question is whether or not we understand the significance of what we are saying. If you ask my children where
Jesus lives, they will point to their chests and say, "Jesus lives in my heart."
To me, that is a great reminder of the importance of clarifying what we are
saying, and not saying, about what we believe.

The Greek word used for heart in Matthew 22:37 is kardia, which among
others things, can mean the center of all physical and spiritual life. It is more
than just the organ pushing blood throughout our physical bodies. When
used in the context of Jesus' statements in Matthew 22, the heart represents the very core of who you are. So, when Jesus says to love Him with
all of your heart, He means that you are to love Him with all that you are. In
His Sermon on the Mount, Jesus emphasized the importance of the heart
by speaking about sin within the heart (Matthew 5:28). The writers of the
Old Testament also consider the importance of the heart (Hebrew word,
leb), as in Psalm 19:14 where David says, "May the words of my mouth and
the meditation of my heart be pleasing to you, O LORD, my rock and my
redeemer."

The centrality of a right heart before God is clearly established in the Bible,
and the call to love the Lord with all of your heart means that this is no
small thing. We are told that the heart is deceitful in Jeremiah 17:1-10, and
David prays for a clean heart before God in Psalm 51. How is it that you are
to love God with all of your heart if your heart is wicked, deceitful and un-
clean? The answer lies in the person and work of Jesus, the Savior. Even in
the Old Testament the idea of a new heart was presented. Ezekiel 36:26-27
records the words of the Lord to the people of Israel. In this passage we are

told, "And I will give you a new heart, and I will put a new spirit in you. I will take out your stony, stubborn heart and give you a tender, responsive heart. And I will put my Spirit in you so that you will follow my decrees and be careful to obey my regulations." The same concept is presented in the New Testament in passages such as Matthew 22,which we have considered, and in passages that indicate a "new man" and a "new creation" in the writings of the apostle Paul (see 2 Corinthians 5:17-21).

PRACTICAL APPLICATION:

Pray for me

In my local church, I volunteer to discuss spiritual issues with parishioners and guests who may have questions regarding spiritual things at the end of each church service. I have experienced all kinds of questions from simply, "Will you pray with me right now that the Lord would make a job available for me this week?" to "Pray for me as I am going through a horrible family situation right now!" I consider every request important because these are issues that are consuming peoples' lives. To them, it is troubling their lives to the point that they have sought out someone at church to discuss and pray about these issues with them.

Try explaining that to a seven-year-old

One of the questions I occasionally receive is, "How can I ask Jesus Christ to save my soul?" I look forward to this question because it is obvious that after hearing the pastor preach about everyone's need for salvation, they've pondered what was said, they've considered what the Bible taught about salvation, and now they want to make a spiritual decision. But one thing I used to find challenging was explaining deep doctrinal terms to young children. So, I took my lead from the best teacher in the world—Jesus Christ—who often used pictures and analogies to make very deep doctrinal concepts understandable.

Don't crash my car

When explaining the spiritual concept of the "heart" to young children, it's a daunting task to help them understand its meaning. You can imagine their confusion when I describe the heart as one's "will" or as "the decision-making, driving force within you that moves you to act, think and trust!" So, I find myself describing "the heart" in simple terms, like comparing the "heart" (i.e., someone's "will") to a familiar memory in a child's life. Many children can relate to the memory of sitting on a parent's lap while he/she drives ever-so-slowly in a parking lot or in their neighborhood, allowing the child to hold on to the steering wheel and direct the car. Of course, the child's legs are not long enough to reach the pedals, so the parent takes care of that responsibility. And, at times, children find a warped sense of pleasure by attempting to turn the car into a near-by mailbox, a long ditch, or in the direction of a flying bird (I am sure many insurance agents can share a lot of colorful stories of similar insurance claims!). When this occurs, the parent immediately places his/her hands on top of the child's hands that are gripping the steering wheel and steers the car into a safe direction—often pulling against the tug of the child who still has his/her sights set on making a hard left turn into the brick wall. The parent immediately applies the brakes, cautions the child and then they continue on their journey.

A picture of great love

Likewise, I explain that when someone "gives their heart to Jesus" it is like jumping into the lap of a parent (i.e., Jesus) and with His guidance, you are allowed to make choices about what you will or won't do. But you need to know that you aren't able to make these choices by yourself (just like you couldn't drive the car all by yourself). You need a lot of help. But God is there , and He lets you sit on His lap so that you can see the road clearly. He is there to hit the gas/brake pedals to gauge the timing of your journey, and He is ever-present to take the steering wheel over in the event you are heading into a ditch. In other words, "giving your heart to Jesus" is accepting the fact that you will always need His help in your life's journey. You commit to trust Jesus to direct your path (Proverbs 3:5-6), and you accept the timing of your journey as coming from the Lord. He knows how fast/slow things should go in your life, and you accept His guidance. When He immediately (and sometimes forcefully) grabs your hands and directs you in a completely different direction, you trust Him just like you trust your parents about things you don't understand yet. As a believer in Jesus Christ, He promises to direct and guide your life out of a tremendous heart of love for you.

> " 'GIVING YOUR HEART TO JESUS' IS ACCEPT-
> ING THE FACT THAT YOU WILL ALWAYS NEED
> HIS HELP IN YOUR LIFE'S JOURNEY. "

It comes down to trust

Every human being must come to the realization that they are unable to see the entire road and that they need to rely upon God to both save their souls and to navigate this life's journey. Don't fear trusting God with your soul and life. Don't fight His loving guidance. There is no shame in trusting God. Frankly, trusting God is a sign of wisdom. Open your "heart" to God and begin experiencing His loving guidance (see the chapter on "Salvation") as you begin to embrace the reality that "We can make our plans, but the LORD determines our steps" (Proverbs 16:9).

Study what the Bible says about the heart
Here are some more verses to read on this topic—Matthew 22:37; Luke 8:11-15; Ezekiel 36; 2 Corinthians 5:17-21.

Write it down...

...& make it HAPPEN!

HUMAN PERSONALITY

(PUR-SUH-NAL-I-TEE)

"Normal life includes the capacity for making decisions, and one is responsible for one's choices. The choice that makes all others more meaningful is commitment to Christ."
- EVANGELICAL DICTIONARY OF THEOLOGY, 1275

The human personality is primarily comprised of three aspects—the intellect, the emotion and the will. These three aspects are involved when a person makes a decision; although every person may use his or her intellect, emotions and will to varying degrees in making those decisions. It is important that you and I process through the way in which we make decisions as well as the way in which we let our intellects and our emotions affect the decisions we make (which is an act of the will).

The intellect of humanity is mentioned throughout the Bible. There are appeals throughout the Bible to the power of thinking and reasoning. The Berean Christians were commended in Acts 17:10-15 for searching the Scriptures and verifying the validity of Paul's message. The very nature of the writing of the Bible was to reveal God to mankind which, in large part, is an intellectual pursuit. Consider the purpose of John's gospel as recorded in John 20:30-31. John says, "The disciples saw Jesus do many other miraculous signs in addition to the ones recorded in this book. But these are written so that you may continue to believe that Jesus is the Messiah, the Son of God, and that by believing in him you will have life by the power of his name." Consider also the appeals to wisdom throughout the book of Proverbs as another example in the Bible of the importance of one's intellect

A person's emotions are also spoken of throughout the Bible. This is seen in many of the narratives in the Bible, and especially in the Psalms. You can sense the passion in the writings such as Psalm 23 or Psalm 150. Deep despair is felt as you read through Psalm 51, which is written in the shadow of moral failure in the life of King David. In the New Testament Jesus is seen as expressing deep emotions when He clears the temple (Mark 11:15-19), and when He weeps at the death of Lazarus (John 11:35).

A person's will is also consistently spoken of in the Bible. Joshua says for the people of Israel to "choose today whom you will serve" (Joshua 24:15). David commits his will in passages such as Psalm 101, where he states what he will and will not do. In the New Testament we see the will being appealed to in verses like Matthew 7:13, where Jesus states that few choose the narrow way. Consistently throughout the Bible the need for right choices is emphasized, both in the Old Testament and the New Testament.

Of the three aspects of the human personality, the most vital part is the will. I say this because the will is the point of decision. The bottom line is that you and I could know the right thing to do (intellectually), we could feel that it is the right decision (emotionally), but until we make a decision to act on the information we receive from our intellect and emotions . . . nothing will happen. #6

PRACTICAL APPLICATION:

What's the difference?
You probably just completed reading the chapter entitled "Heart" and the beginning portion of this chapter on "Human Personality." You might be asking yourself, "What's the difference?" The truth is that "human personality" closely relates to the subject matter of the "heart" in this book. The difference is that whereas the heart is the driving force that moves you to a final decision, there are two influences that strongly affect your decisions—your intellect and emotions. It is necessary to tether your thinking (intellect) to God's truth, so your emotions promote reactions that align with that truth. Once your intellect and emotions are aligned with God's truth, your will" (i.e., "heart") is more likely to make a wise decision that will positively affect your day to day life.

Be yourself
Don't try to mimic someone else's emotions regarding spiritual things. You need to be yourself. While it is true that each person needs to make the same exact choice to accept Jesus Christ as their personal Savior, there is no "right way" to express your appreciation to God when that life-change occurs. So, if you have not yet accepted Christ as your Savior because you may be thinking that you have to somehow react like some other people you've seen, please don't think this way. You may have seen people openly and overtly express their emotions with unhindered abandonment, and that's just not your personality. If you are a reserved person that rarely shows emotion publicly, that's okay. God made you the way you are. You need to be yourself and react according to your God-given personality.

I have had people accept Jesus Christ as their personal Savior and cry tears of joy. And I have talked to others who have accepted Christ as their personal Savior, and they've had totally unemotional expressions on their faces. I actually had one person burst out in laughter after she accepted Christ because her heart was so happy when she made this most vital, life-changing decision. Same decision—different emotions! At the end of the day, your real personality will always emerge. So when you respond to the same spiritual truth that everyone must respond to (i.e., salvation), you are free to experience it through your own personality.

Worship with your heart

If you are a believer in Jesus Christ, don't fall into the temptation to try to express yourself in a church service like everyone else. Be yourself. If you are an introvert, don't feel like you are not as spiritual as those who are comfortable with publicly expressing their emotions. If, when you get moved by the Holy Spirit to worship God in the middle of a song, you prefer to close your eyes and pray rather than shout out words of praise to God, go with it. There is no emotion that is the "correct" emotion to worship God. God listens to your heart and enjoys seeing you express your worship through the God-given personality with which He uniquely knitted you together. Remember Psalm 139:13-14, "You made all the delicate, inner parts of my body and knit me together in my mother's womb. Thank you for making me so wonderfully complex! Your workmanship is marvelous—how well I know it."

> " GOD LISTENS TO YOUR HEART AND ENJOYS SEEING YOU EXPRESS YOUR WORSHIP THROUGH THE GOD-GIVEN PERSONALITY WITH WHICH HE UNIQUELY KNITTED YOU TOGETHER. "

Personality has its limits

But with all these differences, let me rehearse one more time the reality of this truth: While we are all different, we must all come to salvation the exact same way—through confession and repentance of sin to Jesus Christ, believing that the God-man Jesus Christ is the only One able to provide a sufficient atonement (covering) for your sin, and accepting into your heart His invitation to become your Savior (see the chapter on "Salvation"). But after you become a member of God's family (see the chapter on "The Church"), you are free to exhibit your service to God according to your unique and special personality as a testimony of God's beautiful and creative work!

Study what the Bible says about the human personality

Here are some more verses to read on this topic—Joshua 24:15; Psalm 101; Mark 11:15-19; Acts 17:10-15.

Write it down... →

...& make it
HAPPEN!

MATERIAL/IMMATERIAL

(IM-UH-TEER-EE-UHL)

"Then the LORD God formed the man from the dust of the ground. He breathed the breath of life into the man's nostrils, and the man became a living person."
- GENESIS 2:7

There are many questions and considerations when we think about the material and immaterial aspects of mankind. Some believe that in essence mankind is comprised of three distinct substances. This view is called, trichotomy, and it distinguishes between the body, the soul, and the spirit. Another view is called, dichotomy, which argues that the soul and spirit are essentially the same, so the distinction is between the body and the soul/spirit. Still another view is presented which does not distinguish any aspects of mankind. This view holds to an understanding that mankind is essentially one substance. This view is called monism. Proponents of each of these views have passages of Scripture which they use in order to support their claims. For the purposes of our study, it is important to keep in mind the following two points when considering the nature of humanity.

First, the distinction between the material and immaterial aspects of humanity are used throughout Scripture, but in essence, the nature of man should be seen as united. This is not a suggestion that monism is the correct understanding (it seems evident in Scripture that there is a distinction between material and immaterial). But, what I mean by using the term "united" is that the "normal" state of humanity consists of both material and immaterial together in a unity. As the ESV Study Bible mentions, "The separation of the body and soul caused at death is an unnatural tragedy, which will be remedied when the body is resurrected, allowing humans to exist as they were intended to do" (2528). In Genesis 2:7 we are told that, "Then the LORD God formed the man from the dust of the ground. He breathed the breath of life into the man's nostrils, and the man became a living person." In this verse we see both the material and immaterial aspect of mankind being emphasized.

Second, there is a tendency to think of the soul/spirit of a person as being good, and the body as being bad. Although many of us do not take this to the extent of the ascetics, who denied virtually any physical impulses in an effort to please God, we often have a distorted view of both the material and immaterial aspects of humanity. Scripture makes it clear that the entirety of the person was affected by the sin of Adam and Eve in Genesis 3. All of the material and immaterial aspects of mankind are sinful (apart from the saving power of Jesus). Physical impulses and desires should not be viewed as inherently sinful in and of themselves, but should be viewed in the context of humanity being under the curse of sin.

Our understanding of the areas mentioned above becomes very important as we seek to minister to others. If the material aspects of mankind are less important than the immaterial aspects, then do we care about meeting the physical needs of others (food and shelter)? In addition, when we present the gospel message to the person, are we trying to simply save their immaterial aspects, or are we trying to save all of them? The answers to these questions become important as we interact with those both inside the church and those outside the community of believers.

PRACTICAL APPLICATION:

Earn the right to be heard
There is an extremely common axiom that is shared by many people in virtually every sector, discipline, and segment of life—"People don't care how much you know unless they know how much you care!" People will more often take time to listen to what you have to say after you have demonstrated to them that you sincerely care for them as a person.

> " PEOPLE WILL MORE OFTEN TAKE TIME TO LISTEN TO WHAT YOU HAVE TO SAY AFTER YOU HAVE DEMONSTRATED TO THEM THAT YOU SINCERELY CARE FOR THEM AS A PERSON. "

Listen up, Christians!
With all due respect to my fellow believers in Jesus Christ, I feel compelled to say that many Christians do not do a great job at demonstrating their sincere love for people. We sing about it, encourage others to do it, rejoice when we hear of others demonstrating it, but I feel that too few Christians actually engage in the action of touching peoples' lives in a tangible, physical way. We need to be reminded that the very same compassion that our Savior and Lord demonstrated to us needs to be expressed in our interactions with others.

Jesus cared for the spiritual and physical
Jesus Christ Himself demonstrated His love for people before they even knew about His love for them as described in Romans 5:8, "But God showed his great love for us by sending Christ to die for us while we were still sinners." And in a teaching of how much God desires to provide for

His own children, Jesus taught us to consider the needs of people if we sincerely love them in Matthew 7:9, "You parents—if your children ask for a loaf of bread, do you give them a stone instead?" And hours before He was to be arrested in a nearby garden, Jesus made a point to tell His Disciples: "So now I am giving you a new commandment: Love each other. Just as I have loved you, you should love each other. Your love for one another will prove to the world that you are my disciples" (John 13:34-35). Jesus set the example of caring for both the physical and spiritual needs of the people around Him.

Why love?
The purpose of assisting people with their physical needs is to demonstrate the main reason behind your conviction to help them; namely, that Jesus Christ changed your life by giving you the gift of salvation. Therefore, you are exhibiting the same sacrificial love to others in order to resemble the pure love of Jesus Christ. Actions enforce the positive message of the salvation that Jesus Christ can provide if they believe in Him.

They still must choose Jesus
And while is it true that people still have the responsibility to believe God's Word, regardless of being affected by poor examples of Christianity, this statement does recognize that people seem to be more willing to hear God's truth out of the mouth of someone who has first demonstrated their sincere love for him/her in a tangible way. And even though people are not justified in ignoring the message of Jesus Christ because of a negative experience in their lives—every believer ought to strive not to become a hindrance to the life-changing message of how Jesus Christ can save one's soul (see the chapter on "Salvation").

Study what the Bible says about the material-immaterial make up of mankind
Here are some more verses to read on this topic—Genesis 2:7; 1 Thessalonians 5:23; Hebrews 4:12; 1 Corinthians 2:14-3:4; Luke 10:27; Matthew 10:28.

Write it down... ➤

...& make it
HAPPEN!

JESUS CHRIST

ATONEMENT

(UH-TOHN-MUHNT)

"Atonement is the making of enemies into friends by averting the
punishment that their sin would otherwise incur."
- ESV STUDY BIBLE, 2522

#1

In its most basic form, atonement is a covering. In the Old Testament there
is much talk about the covering for the sins of the people of Israel. This
covering was provided by the sacrifice of animals as is seen in passages of
Scripture such as Leviticus 1:4. Every year on one very important day, the
High Priest of the nation of Israel would enter into the Most Holy Place in
the temple and offer a covering (a sacrifice) for his sins, and for the sins of
the nation of Israel. This very special day is called the Day of Atonement
(see Leviticus 16). The Day of Atonement was repeated every year, and the
sacrificial system to provide atonement for the sins of the people was a
repeated occurrence. he word that is used in Leviticus is the Hebrew word,
kapporeth, which means "mercy-seat" or "place of atonement."

#2

In the New Testament the idea of the atonement is carried forward. Christ's
death on the cross provides the atonement for the sins of the world. This
is seen in many passages of Scripture , including the victory that Christ
won through His work on the cross (1 Corinthians 15:55-57), and the price
that Christ paid for our sins (Romans 6:23). One of the best places in the
New Testament to see the significance of the atonement is in the book of
Hebrews. Hebrews 9 and 10 compare the significance of Christ's sacrifice
to the work of the priests in the Old Testament. The Old Testament atoning sacrifices were temporary coverings. As Hebrews 9:11-12 indicates, "So
Christ has now become the High Priest over all the good things that have
come. He has entered that greater, more perfect Tabernacle in heaven,
which was not made by human hands and is not part of this created world.
With his own blood—not the blood of goats and calves—he entered the
Most Holy Place once for all time and secured our redemption forever."

#3

Because of the sin of mankind, there is a broken relationship between God
and mankind. Someone had to step in and make a covering for the sins of
mankind. God took the initiative and made a way for us to be literally saved
from an eternity apart from Him. This salvation has always been through
faith in God. In the Old Testament, salvation was evidenced by the individual's participation in the sacrificial system, which was a shadow of the sacrifice to come in the person and work of Jesus Christ on the cross. We now
have a Great High Priest who entered into the heavens on our behalf to
make atonement (to offer Himself as a covering) for our sins. He did what

the sacrifice of animals could not do and satisfied the demands against you and me once and for all. Unlike the animals, Jesus' atonement on the cross is not a temporary atonement, but a permanent one. He was offered as a spotless sacrifice, without sin, without blemish and without defect.

PRACTICAL APPLICATION:

"You can't find us!"

One of the funniest things I have ever observed my children do when they were young was when we played hide-and-seek in our house. Their hiding spots were so very obvious to me—yet, they thought they were cunning and sly.

We'd start off in the most predictable way:

"Dad, count to 10!"
"Okay," I'd say. Then I would start, "1, 2, 3, 4, 5 . . . "
"No!" They'd exclaim, "Count slower!"
"Okay, I'd reply. And begin counting slower, "1---2---3---"
"No! That's not right. You're forgetting 'Mississippi!'"
With a silent sigh I'd reply, "Okay, with Mississippi."
"1-Mississippi, 2-Mississippi, 3-Mississippi . . . all the way to 10-Mississippi" (which seemed to take forever).

All the while, I could hear them trample around the house and talk to each other so very loudly. Of course, they believed I couldn't hear them. After I finished counting, I'd shout out, "Ready or not, here I come!"

As I walked around, I'd act like I didn't know where they were. Then I'd begin to speak out loud, "I wonder where they are?" "Hmmmm, where could they possibly be?" I repeated these words as I walked to the bedroom where I knew they were hiding . . . because they were so loud! And more often than not, they would not be hiding in the closet, or behind the dresser, or under the bed. Rather, they would be curled up in a ball and hiding underneath the blankets that were on top of the bed.

The closer I would get to the bed, the more difficult it was for them to keep quiet. Little giggles could be heard coming from underneath the blankets after they had tried so hard to contain them. Then my youngest would declare from underneath the covers, "You can't find us. We all covered up!"

Trying to hold back the laughter, I expressed my agreement with her statement, "Boy, I am having the hardest time finding them. I think I'll just lie on this bed and rest for a while before I try to find them." At that moment, I plopped ever-so-carefully on the bed just enough to give them the feeling that I had fallen asleep. Immediately, they would laugh and say, "Get off of us, we're under here!"

"No way!" I'd say. "You were underneath there all this time?"
"Yep!" they would proudly reply. "But you didn't see us because we were all covered up!"

Years pass . . . but hiding place is the same
Even though I can remember being on both sides of that type of hide-and-seek game, I can't help but think that we attempt to hide our sin from God (and everyone else) in the same obvious way. We think that we have effectively masqueraded our sin from everyone (including God), but all the while it is as obvious as hiding underneath blankets on top of a bed.

We attempt to cover our sin by figuring we can outweigh the bad things by performing more charitable deeds in our life. We even attempt to forget our sin and believe that if it is "out-of-sight . . . out-of-mind" in our minds, the same will be true of God. We may even attempt to redefine sin in our minds as "only super bad things" and not what is the accurate definition—"anything that falls short of the glory of God." All of these are poor and obvious hiding places in which to veil the reality that we have sin in our lives.

> " WE MAY EVEN ATTEMPT TO REDEFINE SIN IN OUR MINDS AS "ONLY SUPER BAD THINGS" AND NOT WHAT IS THE ACCURATE DEFINITION— 'ANYTHING THAT FALLS SHORT OF THE GLORY OF GOD.' "

Consider God's covering
The only way a person's sin can be eternally and thoroughly forgiven and "covered" (i.e., atoned for) is to ask God to extend His sinless and sufficient sacrifice (Jesus)and forgive your sins, covering you in His mercy. Then, when others look at you, they will see your life wrapped up in God's mercy. Have you accepted God's atonement for your sin, or are you attempting to cover up your sin in your own creative way? I encourage you to read on in this book—especially the chapters on "Regeneration," "Justification," "Sanctification," "Propitiation" and "Conversion." A more complete explanation of how to apply God's atonement to your life is explained in these chapters.

Rejoice in the change
If you are a believer in Jesus Christ, you should take time every day to celebrate the change that God has made and continues to make in your life. In doing so, you are not focusing all of your attention on the sin that you once committed or still commit, but rather you will celebrate the life-changing

work that God continues to do in your life. God's atonement should be reason for celebration that causes your heart to repeatedly say, "Thank You" to Jesus Christ.

Study what the Bible says about Atonement

Here are some more verses to read on this topic—2 Corinthians 5:21; Leviticus 16:30, 17:11, 23:26-32; Hebrews 7:26-28.

Write it down... ⤳

...& make it
HAPPEN!

REDEMPTION

(RI-DEMP-SHUHN)

"The process by which sinful humans are 'bought back' from the bondage of sin into relationship with God through grace by the 'payment' of Jesus' death. Redemption is one of the pictures or metaphors that the New Testament uses to give insights into God's gracious saving work in Jesus."
- POCKET DICTIONARY OF THEOLOGICAL TERMS, 100-101

The idea expressed with the word redemption is "to buy back" or "to purchase." It is the idea presented in 1 Corinthians 7:23 where the apostle Paul says, "God paid a high price for you, so don't be enslaved by the world." There are three primary Greek words used within the New Testament related to the idea of redemption (agorazō, exagorazō, lytroō). All three of them have the idea of a marketplace. Picture a person traveling to the marketplace and even the concept of a slave market. Romans 6 says that apart from Christ, you and I are slaves to sin, but thankfully Jesus paid the price for our sins and redeemed us.

The Greek word agorazō, is used in 1 Corinthians 6:20 to talk about God buying us with a great price, as at a marketplace. The word, exagorazō, as used in Galatians 3:13, carries with it the idea of rescuing. This means that not only did Jesus pay the price for us, but He rescued us from our situation. The third Greek word used for redemption is lytroō, which is used in Titus 2:14, and it speaks of being released, or freed. By looking at these three words, it is clear that not only did Christ pay the price for our sins (agorazō), but He also removed us from the bondage of our sins (exagorazō), and ultimately has set us free from those sins (agorazō).

It has been said that the story of the Bible could be summarized with the word redemption. From the fall of mankind in the Garden of Eden as recorded in Genesis 3 to mankind spending eternity in the presence of God as recorded in Revelation 20-21, the Bible is a story of God's redemption. One way to speak of the story is to look at what theologians call the metanarrative. A metanarrative is the big picture—the umbrella over the entire story of human history. This grand story of God can be summed up with the four words (1) Creation, (2) Fall, (3) Redemption and (4) Consummation.

God originally created the world, and what He created was "very good" (Genesis 1:31). However, after the creation of the world, sin entered the world when Adam and Eve disobeyed God and ate of the tree of the knowledge of good and evil (Genesis 3). Due to this disobedience, mankind was then separated from God. There was a broken relationship between God and His creation, due not to God's work, but due to mankind's decision to willfully disobey God. But, our study does not end with the consequences of the Fall; the story continues with the redeeming work of Jesus Christ, ultimately costing Him His very life so that you and I could experience an eternity with Him. Second Corinthians 5:19 says, "For God was in Christ, reconciling the world to himself, no longer counting people's sins against them. And he gave us this wonderful message of reconciliation." God has made a way of restoration, a way of reconciliation, a way of redemption through the work of Jesus on the cross.

PRACTICAL APPLICATION:

God bless them
Words cannot express my deep, heart-felt, and sincere appreciation for those who serve in the military and have vowed to protect the citizens of the United States of America. The bravery of these fine men and women make my heart well up with deep gratitude. These people put themselves in harm's way every day to defend the freedoms that every American enjoys today. They are motivated by a deep conviction that this is their purpose in life, and they are committed to fulfill this calling with unequivocal resilience. I am very proud of my fellow Americans serving in the military and their families.

It just takes a second
I have talked with many folks who serve in the military who have seen first-hand the oppression of other governments, and they have told me that it doesn't take long at all to realize how free we really are in America. Some military individuals have freed people from oppression, assisted in humanitarian efforts, observed hostile areas, and have even been a few meters away from the violent attack of an enemy. And all of them have told me that there is nothing like being an American.

It never ends
It refreshes my spirit to hear their stories. But immediately I am reminded that this freedom must be both provided and secured. For if we ever let our guard down, then there is a possibility of losing our freedoms. For the United States, we not only fought to gain our freedom in times past, but we must always remain vigilant to protect our borders every day. Each day, men and women must put their lives in harm's way in order to secure our freedom.

Freedom is not free
Likewise, our spiritual freedom provided by Jesus Christ is afforded to anyone who repents of his/her sins and places their faith in the Lord Jesus

Christ to forgive him/her from their sins (see the chapter on "Salvation"). There must be a point in time when you pause from your busy life and come to realize that you are in spiritual bondage. You can only rely on God and God alone to redeem you from this spiritual bondage. Ephesians 2:1-3 emphasizes that every person is in spiritual bondage:

> "ONCE YOU WERE DEAD BECAUSE OF YOUR DISOBEDIENCE and your many sins. You used to live in sin, just like the rest of the world, obeying the devil—the commander of the powers in the unseen world. He is the spirit at work in the hearts of those who refuse to obey God. All of us used to live that way, following the passionate desires and inclinations of our sinful nature. By our very nature we were subject to God's anger, just like everyone else."

Fortunately, the message of spiritual freedom doesn't stop there—for if it did, we would all be dead spiritually, without hope! Ephesians 2:4-6, 8-9 describes the price that Jesus paid in order to offer us spiritual freedom:

> "BUT GOD IS SO RICH IN MERCY, and he loved us so much, that even though we were dead because of our sins, he gave us life when he raised Christ from the dead. (It is only by God's grace that you have been saved!) For he raised us from the dead along with Christ and seated us with him in the heavenly realms because we are united with Christ Jesus . . .God saved you by his grace when you believed. And you can't take credit for this; it is a gift from God. Salvation is not a reward for the good things we have done, so none of us can boast about it."

Safe and secure

Our spiritual freedom is only as good as the One providing it for us. Fortunately for all believers in Jesus Christ, He promises us that our spiritual freedom is forever secure in Him. Hebrews 7:25 elucidates this promise for all believers:

> THEREFORE HE IS ABLE, ONCE AND FOREVER, TO SAVE those who come to God through him. He lives forever to intercede with God on their behalf.

We are spiritually free from the penalty of our sin (see the chapter on "Justification") as long as Jesus remains alive having been raised from the dead. Fortunately, Hebrews 7:25 assures us that Jesus Christ "lives forever!" Romans 8:33-34 describes how there is no accuser who could ever bring a case against us that could possibly persuade Jesus Christ to release his saving grip upon redeemed souls:

Who dares accuse us whom God has chosen for his own? No one—for God himself has given us right standing with himself. Who then will condemn us? No one—for Christ Jesus died for us and was raised to life for us, and he is sitting in the place of honor at God's right hand, pleading for us.

> **" FORTUNATELY FOR ALL BELIEVERS IN JESUS CHRIST, HE PROMISES US THAT OUR SPIRITUAL FREEDOM IS FOREVER SECURE IN HIM. "**

Is your soul free?

Is your soul free from the bondage of sin? Many people may not feel as if they need freedom, but it is a reality that everyone—regardless of how "better than other people" they feel they are by comparison—their hearts are in need of being released from bondage. Talk to someone who has accepted Christ as their Savior and ask about the time he/she realized their need to be spiritually freed from their sin. Be intentional to reach out to someone who you think needs to consider this decision in his/her life. To reach out to someone about this spiritual issue in your workplace, hometown, church, etc. is both brave and noble . . . and it has eternal value.

Study what the Bible says about redemption

Here are some more verses to read on this topic—John 10:15; Romans 3:24-25, 5:8; 1 Peter 2:24; 1 Corinthians 6:20; Galatians 3:1; Titus 2:14.

Write it down... →

...& make it
HAPPEN!

EIGHTEEN

KENOSIS

(KI-NOH-SIS)

"Though he was God, he did not think of equality with God as something to cling to. Instead, he gave up his divine privileges; he took the humble position of a slave and was born as a human being. When he appeared in human form, he humbled himself in obedience to God and died a criminal's death on a cross."
- PHILIPPIANS 2:6-8

he Greek word used in Philippians 2:7 for the phrase "gave up his divine privileges" is kenoō, which means "to empty." The doctrine of the kenosis is vital to understanding the work of Jesus Christ during His ministry here on earth. Although Jesus is active in the Old Testament (Colossians 1 says that Jesus created the world, and that He sustains the world), Jesus is most fully known by His work during what we call the incarnation. The incarnation is the "word becoming flesh" as seen in John 1:14, and it was the time Jesus was on the earth during His earthly ministry. It was during this time that Jesus emptied Himself, but the question arises in considering Jesus' ministry as to what exactly did Jesus empty Himself of during this time.

The Bible affirms that Jesus is both 100 percent God and 100 percent man. This is evidenced in the fact that Jesus received worship from individuals in the Bible (Matthew 14:33), He forgave sins (Mark 2:5-7), and He called Himself equal to the Father (John 14:9). In addition, throughout the gospel of John, Jesus is seen many times claiming to be the Old Testament "I Am," which is the personal name of God (cf. John 4:26, 6:35, and 14:6). There is a clear reference claiming to be the "I Am" in Exodus 3:14, when Moses was talking to God at the burning bush. But, while He is divine, Jesus also shows His humanity. Jesus was God, yet He became tired and needed to rest (John 4:6 and Mark 4:38). Ultimately, Jesus surrendered His life when He died on the cross. The understanding of Jesus' divinity and humanity are addressed in the doctrine of the kenosis.

Three elements which help to better understand what Christ emptied Himself of are addressed below. These should not be misunderstood to mean that Jesus gave up being God while He was on earth, because being God is His very nature, and He cannot go against His very nature. However, there are things that Jesus did while on earth to ensure that He would be able to accomplish what it was that He came to earth to do. These aspects are listed below:

Jesus surrendered to human limitations
As has already been mentioned, Jesus submitted Himself to the limitations of humanity. He became tired and hungry during His time on earth.

Jesus limited Himself to being at one place at a time during the incarnation
He relied on the Father to perform miracles (Jesus prayed to the Father when raising Lazarus in John 11), although Jesus could have done the miracles through His own power. In addition, Jesus knew only what the Father revealed to Him. This does not mean that Jesus did not have abilities or attributes, but that Jesus submitted to the Father during His time on earth.

Jesus also changed in appearance while on earth
In the book of Revelation, after the incarnation and ascension of Jesus, the apostle John sees Jesus in heaven and describes Him as shining and glorious. While on earth Jesus was humble in appearance. The prophecy of the Messiah in Isaiah 53 says that there "was nothing beautiful or majestic about his appearance, nothing to attract us to him." A glimpse of the glory that accompanies Jesus' appearance is seen in the Mount of Transfiguration, as recorded in Luke 9, but that was not the typical appearance of Jesus on earth.

All this is to say that Jesus humbled Himself when He came to earth, and He made Himself nothing for my sake and for your sake.

PRACTICAL APPLICATION:

I never get tired of going to our favorite vacation spot—Disney World! I never had the chance to go as a child, so now when I take my own family, I think I am more of a kid than they are! Will we ever get tired of going someday? I hope not. Even though many have said the excited emotions of going will wear off, I still look forward with great anticipation for the next time we are able to go. And if I am ever tempted to get tired of going, I think I'll just rehearse all the good times we as a family had there in order to renew my excitement all over again.

Similarly, I don't ever want to lose the excitement about the Kenosis. I encourage you to allow your mind to wallow in the fact that God came to earth in the form of a baby human being in order to provide us with both an example of how to live and to provide Himself as the only sufficient payment for our sins! Let this concept saturate your thinking and eternally boggle your mind. The more you delve into this reality, the more your excitement will last about the reality of God's vast depth and miraculous love He had for you when He came to this earth!

Here are some practical ways in which your understanding of the "Kenosis"

VIRGIN BIRTH

> "The doctrine that holds that the Holy Spirit without the participation of a human father conceived Jesus in the womb of Mary."
> - POCKET DICTIONARY OF THEOLOGICAL TERMS, 120

Roughly 700 years before the birth of Jesus, in Isaiah 7:14 the prophet predicted, "All right then, the Lord himself will give you the sign. Look! The virgin will conceive a child! She will give birth to a son and will call him Immanuel (which means 'God is with us')." The apostle Matthew, in writing his biography of Jesus, indicates that Jesus fulfilled this prophecy of Isaiah in His birth (Matthew 1:22-23). Other accounts of the birth of Jesus also affirm this understanding. Luke 1 records similar terminology, and in verse 34 records Mary's response when the angel Gabriel told her that she would have a son. Mary responded, "But how can this happen? I am a virgin." It seems clear from Scripture that Mary was a virgin when she became pregnant with Jesus.

The significance of the virgin birth is debated at times. What is typically questioned is the actual importance of the doctrine. Some question if Jesus would have needed to be born of a virgin in order to be the Savior of the world. Citing passages of Scripture like Romans 5:12-21, some indicate that Jesus needed to be born of a virgin in order to be sinless. For instance verse 12 is used to suggest that sin passes through the male seed, and therefore Jesus was sinless because He was conceived of the Holy Spirit. Others would argue that there is nothing more inherently sinful between male and female, and that all humanity stands condemned (apart from the saving power of Jesus). Either way, the Bible stresses the significance of the virgin birth of Jesus, which helps to show the significance of the doctrine. Consider the following statement in explaining various aspects of the virgin birth (revised from the Evangelical Dictionary of Theology): "He [Jesus] was conceived in the womb of the Virgin Mary by the power of the Holy Spirit without male seed . . . Jesus was really born; He really became one of us" (1247-1249).

The Bible records the virgin birth as a fact
To question the authenticity of the doctrine is to question Scripture itself. Although you and I may question how and why Jesus was born of a virgin, the fact remains that the Bible says Jesus was born of a virgin.

The virgin birth is a testimony to the supernatural power of God and the supernatural nature of Jesus' life and ministry

There is something unique and very special about Jesus, which is only more emphasized by His birth. The virgin birth helps to solidify in our minds the deity of Jesus.

The virgin birth also establishes the humanity of Jesus
Mary was literally the mother of God. As the Evangelical Dictionary of Theology states in explaining various aspects of the virgin birth, "He [Jesus] was conceived in the womb of the Virgin Mary by the power of the Holy Spirit without male seed . . . Jesus was really born; He really became one of us."

The doctrine of the virgin birth helps you and I understand the sinlessness of Jesus
Because of the fall of mankind (as recorded in Genesis 3), you and I are born into sin, but there is something very special and very unique about the birth of Jesus. He was conceived of the Virgin Mary, and He lived a life without sin (2 Corinthians 5:21 and 1 John 3:5).

PRACTICAL APPLICATION:

The virgin conception and birth of Jesus Christ was nothing short of a miracle. But it was a miracle among miracles. Matthew 1:18 begins a clear and exact description of Jesus Christ with the words, "This is how Jesus the Messiah was born." The remainder of the chapter describes how God commands angelic beings for His own purpose, how the event fulfilled prophecies that were uttered centuries before the event, how God orchestrated His own entry to earth perfectly to how He had foretold is birth through His prophets in the Old Testament, how evil people attempted to end His life as a toddler, and how even the traveling schedule of the baby Jesus and His parents perfectly aligned with afore told prophecies. John 1:3, 4, 14 continues the list of miracles—noting that the baby that Mary delivered was the very God who created the entire world before time began.

This unique event had no parallel in history and will have no replicator in the future. This unique event, though extremely difficult to understand per our human thinking, is evidence of the unique nature of Jesus Christ. For it was necessary to be conceived miraculously by the Holy Spirit in order to have a unique, sinless nature. And it was this sinless nature of the God-man, Jesus Christ that would make Him the only person able to redeem mankind from their sinfulness.

He's way over my head
The reality of the virgin birth of Jesus Christ should cause all believers in Jesus Christ to rest assured that God's ways are better than our ways! The prophet Isaiah said it best in Isaiah 55:8-9, "'My thoughts are nothing like your thoughts,' says the LORD. 'And my ways are far beyond anything

you could imagine. For just as the heavens are higher than the earth, so my ways are higher than your ways and my thoughts higher than your thoughts.'"

Trust the ways of God

Think of a time where you could not understand why certain things went the way they did . . . and they didn't go the way you thought they should. Can you think of a plan that was changed, and you wondered why it didn't go your way? Or, the opportunity you didn't get after being excited about it for a long time? Or, maybe you had expressed your feelings towards someone that were not reciprocated? It is at these times that trust in the miracle-performing God must take over your thinking. Yes, it is hard to be disappointed after we get all pumped up emotionally about an idea or set our sights on an opportunity. The more we think about our dreams the more we begin to believe that they should happen.

Trust the timing of God

I want to encourage you to make room in your thinking to accept God's intervention with every plan you make. Be postured and ready to say, "Okay, God, I see You want me to go in a different direction, so I'll go back to the drawing board. There is a biblical Proverb that emphasizes that we should make our plans while at the same time be willing to concede to God's ultimate plan for our lives. Proverbs 16:9 says, "We can make our plans, but the LORD determines our steps."

> " I WANT TO ENCOURAGE YOU TO MAKE ROOM IN YOUR THINKING TO ACCEPT GOD'S INTERVENTION WITH EVERY PLAN YOU MAKE. "

It takes discipline

It takes some real spiritual discipline to say, "Okay God, You have demonstrated Your power so convincingly in the past—as in Your virgin birth 2000 years ago and all the subsequent miracles—I will trust that You know what You are doing today!" Difficult? Yes. Necessary? Absolutely. Without reflecting on the miracles of God and His providential plan in life, we are left to only our best guess as to how to negotiate life. But trusting God and His perfect timing also takes a lot of pressure off of a believer's life. You don't have to be God. You don't have to worry about orchestrating every single thing in your life. You simply have to work on doing one thing—to trust God—the same God who has performed amazing miracles in so many lives. Will you trust Him to take care of the details of your life?

Study what the Bible says about the virgin birth of Jesus Christ

Here are some more verses to read on this topic—Matthew 1:18, 22-25; Luke 1:26-28; Isaiah 7:14; Romans 5:12-21; John 1:1-18.

Write it down... ⟶

...& make it
HAPPEN!

RESURRECTION

(REZ-UH-REK-SHUHN)

"The central, defining doctrine and claim of the Christian faith is the resurrection of Jesus Christ, whom God brought forth from the dead. The resurrection of the dead refers to the promise based on the bodily resurrection of Jesus, that all believers will one day join Christ in the resurrection. Believers will be transformed, that is, renewed both morally and physically with 'spiritual' bodies adapted for eternal life with God."
- POCKET DICTIONARY OF THEOLOGICAL TERMS, 102

More than anything else, Christianity is based on the resurrection of Jesus Christ. It is the central claim of our theology. The apostle Paul says in 1 Corinthians 15:17, "If Christ has not been raised, then your faith is useless and you are still guilty of your sins." He acknowledges the centrality of the doctrine of the resurrection to the Christian faith. There is much debate about the resurrection, due in part to the great significance the doctrine has for Christianity. Opponents of Christianity know that without the resurrection, there is no Christianity.

The Greek word for resurrection is anastasis, meaning "a rising up." In the context of the person of Jesus Christ, it includes more than just a renewal of life to the former being. Jesus' resurrected body was in some ways the same as the body that went into the grave, and in some ways it was different. At times Jesus was recognized, and at other times He was not recognized (Luke 24:13-32). This is likely an indication of the future resurrection of those who follow Jesus.

The importance of the resurrection is seen in three broad areas. First, it is recognition of the supernatural work of God. Many individuals in the world live as though there is not a God to be accountable to, but recognition of the resurrection of Jesus is an indication that an individual realizes their finiteness and limitations. If there is a God, then you and I are accountable to that God. Belief in the resurrection is an indication of the realization of accountability to God.

The resurrection affirms the teaching and ministry of Jesus. It is as though the resurrection is the stamp of approval by the heavenly Father. Jesus made some amazing claims throughout His ministry. He received worship from people, He claimed to be equal with the heavenly Father, He claimed to forgive sins, and He even claimed that He would be raised from the dead. The resurrection of Jesus is confirmation of the ministry and claims of Jesus.

The resurrection of Jesus also points to the future resurrection of those who trust in Him. It motivates believers and gives them strength to live for Him in the present age. When speaking of the significance of the resurrection, the ESV Study Bible indicates, "The resurrection is not merely a doctrine to be affirmed intellectually; it is the resounding affirmation that Jesus reigns over all, and the power that raised Him from the dead is the Christian's power for living the Christian life on earth and the assurance of eternal life in heaven" (2525-2526). According to 1 Corinthians 15:53, our dying bodies will be transformed into bodies that will never die. Because of the resurrection of Jesus, you and I can have complete confidence in His saving power. Jesus literally won victory over death in His resurrection.

Finally, it is important to understand the resurrection of Jesus as a bodily resurrection, not merely a spiritual resurrection. Paul's statements in 1 Corinthians 15 can best be understood within the context of a physical, personal resurrection. It is the hope in which Paul instructs us to have comfort. In addition, the appearances of Christ after the resurrection indicate a bodily resurrection. He ate and He welcomed the apostles to touch His scars. These are just a couple examples of physical activities in which Jesus participated after the resurrection.

PRACTICAL APPLICATION:

Every person who has become a true believer in Jesus Christ will celebrate His resurrection as the foundational evidence that what Jesus Christ said about Himself was indeed true (i.e., that He was God Himself, the only One able to forgive the sins of mankind, the spiritual protector of all who place their faith in Him, etc.). This can be said of every true believer because the Bible states clearly that unless a person believes that Jesus Christ resurrected from the dead (i.e., physically, after being killed on the cross), they are unable to be labeled as a believer in Jesus Christ. Romans 10:9 clearly states this reality, "If you confess with your mouth that Jesus is Lord and believe in your heart that God raised him from the dead, you will be saved."

So, what should the resurrection cause us to do as believers other than provide assurance that our salvation has a firm and unswerving foundation in Jesus Christ? The apostle Paul answered that very question in one of the most vivid chapters in the Bible. In 1 Corinthians chapter 15, there are fifty-eight verses. The first fifty-seven verses discuss the great reality of the resurrection of Jesus Christ. The last verse in the chapter provides what our reaction should be to this fantastic teaching on the resurrection of Jesus Christ: "So, my dear brothers and sisters, be strong and immovable. Always work enthusiastically for the Lord, for you know that nothing you do for the Lord is ever useless" (1 Corinthians 15:58).

Taken directly from 1 Corinthians 15:58, there are four practical ways in which the reality of the resurrection of Jesus Christ can affect your life in a God-honoring way today:

1. Clip your wings

Just as a bird's wings can be clipped in order to restrict its flight, take time to clip out of your life whatever would tempt you to fly outside of God's safe perimeters for your life. This is exactly what the apostle Paul intended when he wrote, "So, my dear brothers and sisters, be strong and immovable . . . " In light of the resurrection of Jesus Christ, the apostle Paul simply encourages you to "render yourself immobile" spiritually. In other words, be strong enough and committed enough to do whatever it takes to stay within the protective realm of God's Word. If you have placed your entire life upon the reality that Jesus Christ has risen from the dead, then you should be equally committed to trust God in the day-to-day decisions in life.

> **NOTICE THE WORD "ENTHUSIASTICALLY." THIS IS A KEY WORD AS IT PORTRAYS THE RIGHT HEART ATTITUDE THAT ALL BELIEVERS SHOULD HAVE ABOUT OBEYING AND SERVING GOD.**

2. Be enthusiastically active for God

After encouraging every believer to remain in the will of God, the apostle Paul then instructs us to, "Always work enthusiastically for the Lord . . . " It follows logically that if God did all of this for us, then out of an enthusiastically grateful heart we should want to serve Him in any way possible! Notice the word "enthusiastically." This is a key word as it portrays the right heart attitude that all believers should have about obeying and serving God. No believer who has truly grasped the awesome reality of the resurrection of Jesus Christ will view the commands, directives, and encouragements from God as meaningless and restrictive do's-and-don'ts. Rather, every believer should enthusiastically welcome them as spiritual guidance from an amazingly gracious God!

3. Live with no regrets

In this profound chapter on the reality of the resurrection of Jesus Christ, the final phrase emphasizes that no believer should ever regret serving the same God Who—came to earth, lived a sinless life, was crucified and rose again from the dead to provide forgiveness of our sins and salvation of our souls. If you are a believer in Jesus Christ, ". . . know that nothing you do for the Lord is ever useless." Do not spend

SALVATION

REGENERATION

(RI-JEN-UH-REY-SHUHN)

"Regeneration, or new birth, is an inner re-creating of fallen human nature by the gracious sovereign action of the Holy Spirit (John 3:5-8)."
- EVANGELICAL DICTIONARY OF THEOLOGICAL TERMS, 1000

In John 3, Jesus is recorded as having a conversation with Nicodemus. According to church tradition, Nicodemus was a very wealthy and powerful individual within Jerusalem. In addition, Nicodemus was a member of the Pharisees, the recognized religious leaders of the nation of Israel. During this conversation Jesus told Nicodemus that "you must be born again." The apostle John notes the confusion that Nicodemus experienced by Jesus' statement, as Nicodemus tried to understand how a person could be born a second time. Nicodemus was thinking of a physical re-birth, but Jesus spoke of a rebirth from above, or a spiritual re-birth. This concept of a spiritual re-birth is what is known as regeneration.

#1

The idea of regeneration is found throughout the Bible. The Old Testament speaks of the idea of regeneration in passages such as Deuteronomy 10:16 where the readers are told that they need a circumcision of their hearts. Or perhaps the essence of regeneration is most clearly seen in Ezekiel 36:22-32, when the nation of Israel is told that God will replace their heart of stone with a heart of flesh. The ideas of Ezekiel 36 deal with the broader area of salvation, and specifically the new life of regeneration.

There are three important things to keep in mind concerning the concept of regeneration:

Only God can bring new life
Scripture contains many examples of individuals trying to work their way to God. The saving work of salvation is the work of God, alone; it is a work from above. Ezekiel 37 is another example of this new life from above. In this passage of Scripture Ezekiel prophesies over a valley of dry bones, and the bones come to life because of the Spirit of God. In the same way, the Spirit of God brings new life to us at salvation.

We respond by repentance and faith #2
The individual's response to God's working in salvation is our repentance and faith in the saving work of God. These two components (repentance and faith) could be viewed as salvation from the perspective of the individual, and it's known as the concept of conversion. Romans 10:9-10 indicates

that to be saved, we must confess and believe in the Lord Jesus Christ. Regeneration, however, is salvation from the perspective of God.

The concept of regeneration is evidenced throughout the Bible
As I have mentioned, the Bible contains the idea of regeneration in many places, but it is important to keep in mind that the word itself is rarely used in the Bible. The Greek word is paliggenesia and means "new life" or "renewal." It is only found in Titus 3:5 and Matthew 19:28, but the concept of regeneration is found many places. Titus 3:5 (NASB) states, "He saved us, not on the basis of deeds which we have done in righteousness, but according to His mercy, by the washing of regeneration [He washed away our sins] and renewing by the Holy Spirit." The new life that God brings about is truly an amazing act of His graciousness and love.

PRACTICAL APPLICATION:

Take a bath
On the last evening before He was to be captured, beaten and ultimately crucified, Jesus had a final meal with His closest friends. During this meal, He stood up from the table and performed a task that only servants were expected to do—not Rabbis or their disciples. Jesus washed off the dirt that was on the feet of the dinner guests, dirt they had accumulated on their journey to the house.

Jesus' friends were astounded at what He was doing. Some allowed Him to do so, but one friend objected. His name was Peter. "No," Peter protested, "you will never ever wash my feet" (John 13:8a)! To which Jesus replied, "Unless I wash you, you won't belong to me" (John 13:8b). So, Peter surmises that if getting "washed" by Jesus is what he needs, then he wants an entire bath—not just his feet washed! "Simon Peter exclaimed, 'Then wash my hands and head as well, Lord, not just my feet!'" But Jesus finally cut through Peter's confusion and explained the meaning of His actions. Jesus replied, 'A person who has bathed all over does not need to wash, except for the feet . . .'" (John 13:10a). Jesus was giving the disciples a visual illustration to describe the relationship of "regeneration by Jesus" (bathed all over)and "daily fellowship with Him" (washing the feet).

Jesus taught that once you are truly saved (see the chapter on "Salvation"), you will not need to ask Jesus to save you again. Jesus likened this to taking a bath. Once you have been washed, you don't need to get washed all over again. But Jesus was saying that when a cleanly-washed person walks down a dusty road—in sandals—they do need to have their feet occasionally cleaned. In this analogy, the bath is "regeneration" and the feet cleaning is "fellowship with Jesus" or "forgiveness of daily sins that hinder our fellowship and communion with our Savior." Regeneration is what God does in "washing" you completely! Asking Him through prayer to "wash your feet" is to ask Him to forgive you of your sinful thoughts or actions that were unbecoming in a regenerated person.

Regeneration should produce gratitude

Just as when we receive a precious gift that causes us to offer a huge "thanks" in return, the gift of regeneration should cause our hearts to desire to thank God with our words, thoughts, deeds and actions. As we saw earlier in Titus 3:5, God did a pretty amazing miracle in offering regeneration to us. It is only because of His mercy and grace that He saves us and gives us new life—not because of who we are or what we have done.

> **JUST AS WHEN WE RECEIVE A PRECIOUS GIFT THAT CAUSES US TO OFFER A HUGE 'THANKS' IN RETURN, THE GIFT OF REGENERATION SHOULD CAUSE OUR HEARTS TO DESIRE TO THANK GOD WITH OUR WORDS, THOUGHTS, DEEDS AND ACTIONS.**

When we understand how hopeless our souls were to obtain salvation on our own, the more likely we will not receive God's instructions as strict rules from an insensitive God. Rather, we will see His instructions as protective guardrails, and we will appreciate the security we find in walking through each day with Him.

Regeneration should make you want to keep your feet clean

When you, as a believer, really understand what Jesus did when He offered you "regeneration" (i.e., "salvation"), it makes you desire to stay in close fellowship with Him, not wanting to dishonor Him by your sinful words, thoughts, deeds or actions.

Regeneration is not "rejuvenation"

God changed us when He regenerated us. He didn't just resuscitate our sinful souls, He washed our souls clean and gave us a new life. It doesn't mean we will not still sin and fall short of His glory while we are living in this world (that won't happen until we are in heaven with Jesus Himself someday). But it does mean that we now have the power over sin, and we don't have to sin anymore—it's a moment by moment choice. All of this is because of what God did to regenerate our souls!

I encourage you to read and meditate over one of the most vivid descriptions of what God did for us in regeneration:

EPHESIANS 2:1-10

[1] Once you were dead because of your disobedience and your many sins. [2] You used to live in sin, just like the rest of the world, obeying the devil—the commander of the powers in the unseen world. He is the spirit at work in the hearts of those who refuse to obey God. [3] All of us used to live that way, following the passionate desires and inclinations of our sinful nature. By our very nature we were subject to God's anger, just like everyone else. [4] But God is so rich in mercy, and he loved us so much, [5] that even though we were dead because of our sins, he gave us life when he raised Christ from the dead. (It is only by God's grace that you have been saved!) [6] For he raised us from the dead along with Christ and seated us with him in the heavenly realms because we are united with Christ Jesus. [7] So God can point to us in all future ages as examples of the incredible wealth of his grace and kindness toward us, as shown in all he has done for us who are united with Christ Jesus. [8] God saved you by his grace when you believed. And you can't take credit for this; it is a gift from God. [9] Salvation is not a reward for the good things we have done, so none of us can boast about it. [10] For we are God's masterpiece. He has created us anew in Christ Jesus, so we can do the good things he planned for us long ago.

Study what the Bible says about regeneration
Here are some more verses to read on this topic—1 Peter 1:23; Ephesians 2:1-10; Titus 3:4-7; John 3:3-8.

Write it down...

...& make it
HAPPEN!

JUSTIFICATION

(JUHS-TUH-FI-KEY-SHUHN)

"Question: What is justification? Answer: Justification is an act of God's free grace, wherein He pardoneth all our sins, and accepteth us as righteous in His sight, only for the righteousness of Christ imputed to us, and received by faith alone."
- WESTMINSTER SHORT CATECHISM   *#3*

To be justified is to be "declared righteous." I have heard it said that to be justified is to be just-as-if-I'd never sinned. This definition may be an easy way to remember the definition, but unfortunately it is not an accurate representation of the biblical meaning of the word, justified. From a biblical perspective, the word justified means to be "declared righteous." It is actually a legal term which is used in Scripture, and it relates more to our position before Christ than our experiences here on earth. Wayne Grudem, in Bible Doctrine, defines justification as, "An instantaneous legal act of God in which he (1) thinks of our sins as forgiven and Christ's righteousness as belonging to us, and (2) declares us to be righteous in his sight" (488). *#4*

The meaning of the word took on new significance for me after talking to two lawyer friends of mine. They explained that from a legal standpoint a defendant can be found "not guilty" of a crime, but that does not mean that the defendant is "innocent." In a similar way, all people have been condemned as guilty before God; we are certainly not innocent. The Bible tells us that it is because of our sin that we will eventually die. But, the good news of the message of the Bible is that Jesus willingly gave His life on our behalf, even when we were in our own sins (Romans 5:8).

One of the key biblical passages explaining the significance of justification is found in 2 Corinthians 5. In verse 21, the apostle Paul explains that the sinless Jesus took on our sins so that we, as sinners, would be able to be righteous (justified) in Jesus. The actual Greek word is dikaiosynē, which indicates that a person is in a right position with God. It is the heart of the gospel, and it is the message that Christians are called to proclaim. Other extremely important passages about God's righteousness and justification are found throughout the book of Romans. The apostle Paul demonstrates how all people stand condemned before a Holy God, and that no one is righteous (Romans 3:10). However, salvation is offered through the work of Jesus Christ. While we were still in our sins, Jesus died on our behalf (Romans 5:8). This amazing thought is seen in Romans 3:23-24. Verse 23 says that all have sinned, but verse 24 says that we have been "freely justified" (NKJV) by the grace of God. What an awesome truth to consider.

Another point to consider is that the doctrine of justification is a concept that should be understood as being instantaneous. By that I mean that in an instant a person is declared righteous. Although there may be a process that leads up to that moment, there is a definitive point in time where a person goes from being condemned by God (an enemy of God) to being declared righteous by God (a child of God). Not by anything that we have done, but by the saving power of Jesus and the graciousness of God.

PRACTICAL APPLICATION:

In a sermon preached by the late Rev. E.V. Hill in a church in Illinois, he made a simple yet profound point (paraphrased):

> "YOU MAY HAVE POLITICAL PEACE, economic peace, social peace, familial peace—all kinds of peace. But there may be someone here today sitting under the sound of my voice who does not have the certainty that you have peace with God."

Justification does not imply that we will never make mistakes. We most certainly will. Fortunately, justification provides the certainty that those mistakes do not carry the weight to discharge you out of the loving membership of God's family. Once you are justified by God, you have been pardoned from bearing the penalty of that sin. Thus, the mistakes and sins you commit after you have been justified should serve as a humbling reminder that until you are in heaven with God and absent from the very influence of sin, you will be endlessly tempted to bring dishonor to the gracious Lord Who justified your soul. Even though your soul has been justified, you need to constantly ask the Lord to forgive you for not acting like who you really are on the inside—a child of God.

There is not a day that goes by that I don't think about the fact that I am at peace with God. At the same time, there is not a day that goes by that I don't recognize something in my life that could be improved upon so as to show my gratitude to God for saving my soul.

Here are four practical ways in which your understanding of "justification" can affect your life in a God-honoring way:

1. Walk down memory lane
Take a moment each week to think about what your life would be like if the Lord would not have justified your heart. This spiritual reminiscing will serve as a continual reminder of the truly miraculous power of God. Be careful not to become desensitized to the change that God has made in your life. And even if your heart says, "But wait! Why would I always want to reopen past wounds?" That's not the recommendation here . Do not rehearse the sordid details of your past, but rather focus

> **EVEN THOUGH YOUR SOUL HAS BEEN JUS-TIFIED, YOU NEED TO CONSTANTLY ASK THE LORD TO FORGIVE YOU FOR NOT ACTING LIKE WHO YOU REALLY ARE ON THE INSIDE—A CHILD OF GOD.**

upon God's gracious power, mercy, love and forgiveness that forever changed your life. Remember this common principle: "You cannot change the past, but you can change the meaning of it!"

2. Get back on track every night
Don't let your head hit the pillow without taking a moment to remember how far you have come with God's help. If you can daily refresh your spiritual perspective about your life, it can be a powerful motivator to never go down that road again. Revelation 2:5a emphasizes this practice when it says, "Look how far you have fallen! Turn back to me and do the works you did at first." In this verse you see the directive to remember ("Look how far you have fallen!"), repent ("Turn back to me"), and practice God-honoring attitudes ("do the works you did at first").

3. Rest when others are anxious
This world is full of anxiety. Current events make many people nervous about "what might happen next" or "is it all going to end," etc. While there is certainly a mandate to be good managers of what the Lord has given us to oversee (e.g., family, finances, jobs, relationships, etc.), we ought not to be overly anxious about the "unknowns" of life. Justification gives us assurance that we know Who holds our eternal fate secure. So, focus on the universal truths of which God assures us—namely, Who God is and what He has done for us through justifying our souls. And if He can safely coddle our eternal soul in His hands, then we can trust Him to direct our paths in this world full of unknowns.

4. Share your secret
Once you really grasp the amazingly gracious gift of God in justification, it seems only natural to want to share your story of life-change with others. Just follow the simple instructions Jesus Himself told a man who had just experienced forgiveness from his sins, ". . . go home to your family, and tell them everything the Lord has done for you and how merciful he has been" (Mark 5:19).

Study what the Bible says about justification
Here are some more verses to read on this topic—Ephesians 2:8; Romans 3:21-26; 8:30-33; Colossians 3:13-15.

Write it down... →

...& make it
HAPPEN!

SANCTIFICATION

(SANGK-TUH-FAH-KEY-SHUHN)

"A progressive work of God and man that makes us more and more free from sin and like Christ in our actual lives."
- WAYNE GRUDEM, Bible Doctrine, 493

To be sanctified is to be "set apart," which carries with it the idea of holiness. The concept is seen throughout both the Old Testament and the New Testament, and it often has both positive and negative aspects. The term itself can be related to people, places, or even specific things. For our purposes we will focus on the significance of the concept for individuals. In a positive sense, the individual who is sanctified is to be "set apart" for God. Individuals are to be set apart so that God can work uniquely through each one of them. The nation of Israel was to be set apart for God, so that the entire nation could be an example for the rest of the world. Deuteronomy 7:6 records God speaking to the nation of Israel and saying that they were to be a holy (sanctified) people. If the positive aspect of sanctification is that an individual is to be set apart for God, then from a negative viewpoint the person should be set apart from evil. To be holy—to be righteous—is to turn from sin. Paul reminds Timothy to run from youthful lusts and to pursue righteousness in 2 Timothy 2:22.

Consider the concept of sanctification as seen in the Old Testament. The Hebrew word that is used is qadowsh. It means to be holy, to be set apart, or to be sacred. Leviticus 20:26 uses this term to describe God, and also to indicate that we are to be holy. The call of Isaiah in Isaiah 6:5 shares a similar idea when Isaiah cries out, "It's all over! I am doomed, for I am a sinful man. I have filthy lips, and I live among a people with filthy lips. Yet I have seen the King, the LORD of Heaven's Armies."

In the New Testament the same concept is seen in the Greek word hagios, which means a holy thing or a saint. 1 Peter 1:15 shares the same idea as Leviticus 20:26 about the need to be holy. The church (the assembly of the followers of Jesus), is said to be sanctified in Ephesians 5:25-27, which is accomplished through the work of Jesus. Many other New Testament passages echo the same idea. It is even found in the way the apostle Paul addresses the Christians to whom he writes his letters. His typical greeting is addressed to the "saints." For examples, see Romans 1:7 (NASB) or Ephesians 1:1 (NASB).

One additional consideration to keep in mind is that sanctification is an ongoing process. It is important to remember that God is helping us with our weaknesses, and that He continually is working to make us more like Jesus. Many theologians talk about three aspects to sanctification. At the time of conversion the individual is "set apart" to God (this is something that has hopefully happened in your past). After salvation, sanctification is an ongoing process that will be continued throughout this life (this is the present aspect of sanctification). Eventually we will be with Jesus in heaven, and at that point we will be entirely set apart to God (this is something in the future). So, concerning sanctification, you will notice the discussion focusing on either the past, present or future aspects of the doctrine, which affects the way in which we should interpret a particular passage of Scripture.

> **❝ IT IS IMPORTANT TO REMEMBER THAT GOD IS HELPING US WITH OUR WEAKNESSES, AND THAT HE CONTINUALLY IS WORKING TO MAKE US MORE LIKE JESUS. ❞**

PRACTICAL APPLICATION:

Have you ever had someone passionately appeal to you to join a community, a club, or an event? And after you had given it a lot of thought you finally agreed. Then, leading up to the first day you would meet everyone, you began to actually get excited about meeting new people, making new friends and learning more about this new community that you agreed to join. But when you arrived at the big event, the person who pleaded with you to join simply greeted you at the door with a smile, expressed how glad he/she was to see you, directed you to the refreshment table, and then walked away and never spoke to you again the rest of the night! You were left to your own ingenuity to learn more about the people around you, navigating the social waters all alone. Without warning, you had to be pro-active in engaging people at the event rather than others engaging you first. Later that evening, however, you found some consolation when you saw your friend doing the same thing to the other "recruits" that he/she had pleaded with to join the same community!

I too have experienced this scenario a few times in my life. And every time it happened, it made me ask questions like, "Did that person really care for me as a friend? Or, was he/she just interested in meeting a quota of recruits, but didn't really care for me as a person?" Fortunately, this is NOT how God treats those who have made the decision to accept Jesus Christ as their personal Savior.

At the point of salvation (i.e., justification), God promises to never leave you alone. And unlike an uncaring host at a party who is concerned simply with how many people are filling up a room, God is personally concerned with how you mature spiritually, and how your feelings and emotions develop as you travel this spiritual journey. At the very moment you surrender your will to His saving grace and love, He promises to "never leave you nor forsake you" (Deuteronomy 31:6, 8; Joshua 1:5; 1 Kings 8:57; 1 Chronicles 28:20; Psalm 27:9; Jeremiah 18:14; Hebrews 13:5). This spiritual concern and mentoring that God provides every follower of Christ is called "sanctification."

Sanctification is a label used by many to describe how God the Holy Spirit begins to speak, teach and guide every believer in Jesus Christ now that the Holy Spirit dwells within the believer's heart. Sometimes God will use conviction to cause a believer to pause from making a decision that would potentially dishonor God and harm the believer. Other times, God impresses upon a person's heart to obey God rather than follow the counsel of another person. There are also times where God aligns His guidance with His own Word, the Bible. That is how every believer knows if the guidance is coming from God or their own thinking—if the believer's heart is compelled to act or think in such a way that aligns perfectly with the Bible's teachings. Therefore, the foundation to all spiritual maturity is a believer's life is the Holy Scriptures.

And fortunately, God promises that this level of attention, love and guidance will never end in your life as a believer in Jesus Christ. "And I am certain that God, who began the good work within you, will continue his work until it is finally finished on the day when Christ Jesus returns" (Philippians 1:6).

In light of God's commitment to you, you must also do your part to welcome His perfect guidance. Here are some spiritual steps you can take in order to experience God's perfect guidance:

#5

1. Don't ignore the guidance of God
Always be open to what God has to say to you at the moment He wishes to guide you in a particular area. It may seem like awkward timing—or flat out horrible timing—to you, but trust the heart of God Who has promised to "never leave you nor forsake you!"

2. Remain sensitive to the guidance of God
Simply put, the more you obey God, the more sensitive you will be to His guidance. The more you dishonor God with your actions and thoughts, the more desensitized you will be to His vital spiritual guidance.

3. Read daily and pray always
The Bible is here for our sanctification. It contains the foundation upon which all decisions, thoughts and deeds should be scrutinized. So, read and meditate upon His Holy Word to you every day. And pray throughout

the day, remembering what you have read and ask this request of God—
"Mature me today."

4. Don't strive to be a spiritual superhero overnight

This goal will only discourage you. Like an expert physical trainer, God will push you, prompt you, instruct you and, if necessary, "get in your face" to motivate you to do what you need to do in order to become stronger in your faith. But the objective is to become stronger today than you were yesterday. This is progress to be proud of. So, strive for day-to-day sanctification . . . growing a little more every day.

Study what the Bible says about sanctification

Here are some more verses to read on this topic—1 Corinthians 1:18; Romans 6:17-18; 2 Corinthians 3:18, 7:1; Philippians 3:21; Leviticus 20:26.

Write it down...→

...& make it
HAPPEN!

TWENTY FOUR

PROPITIATION

(PRUH-PISH-EE-EY-SHUHN)

"An offering that turns away the wrath of God directed against sin.
According to the New Testament, God has provided the offering
that removes the divine wrath, for in love the Father sent the Son
to be the propitiation (or atoning sacrifice) for
human sin (1 John 4:10)"
- POCKET DICTIONARY OF THEOLOGICAL TERMS, 96

Because of the sin of mankind (see Genesis 3), mankind is separated from
God. But, before the story gets better, it gets worse. Not only is there a
separation between us and God, mankind is actually in opposition to God—
to the point where God's wrath burns against you and me. We are told in
the Bible that we cannot do anything to earn our way to a right relationship
with God. If anyone would have been a candidate for earning salvation, it
would have been the apostle Paul. In Philippians 3 Paul recounts his "righteousness" according to his own abilities. He mentions that he was born of
the right family, in the right nation, had the right vocation, and diligently
followed the rules of his religion. However, he continues in his message to
say that all of these things are meaningless apart from Jesus. He recognizes
that these things do not bring about true righteousness—righteousness
from the one true God. He understands that apart from the salvation of
Jesus, he is destined to experience the wrath of God.

That is where the good news of the gospel comes into play (the word
gospel means "goods news"). You and I are destined for destruction—no
matter how good our family is, and no matter how good we try to serve
God with our own abilities. We are destined for the wrath of God unless
someone intervenes. Romans 1:18 says, "But God shows his anger from
heaven against all sinful, wicked people who suppress the truth by their
wickedness." This means that all of humanity is under the condemnation of
sin and destined for the wrath of God.

But, the story does not end with you and me paying the price for our own
sins. The story does not end without hope. The selfless act of Jesus on the
cross satisfied the demands of the law. Jesus' sacrifice paid the price

" THOSE WHO FOLLOW JESUS FOLLOW A SAV-
IOR WHO TRULY PAID THE ULTIMATE PRICE
SO THAT WE COULD HAVE ETERNAL LIFE WITH
HIM. "

for our sins. The biblical word for this satisfaction is the word propitiation. The Greek word is hilasmos, meaning "an appeasing." Jesus appeased the wrath of God when He died on the cross. 1 John 4:10 says, "This is real love—not that we loved God, but that he loved us and sent his Son as a sacrifice to take away our sins." The word propitiation is only used a couple times in the New Testament (see also 1 John 2:2 NASB; Romans 3:25 NASB; Hebrews 2:17 NASB), but the concept is seen all throughout the New Testament. It is the emphasis in the work of Jesus on the cross, and it is the focus point of the gospel. Perhaps the best representation of the idea of propitiation is in 2 Corinthians 5:21. As the apostle Paul says, "For God made Christ, who never sinned, to be the offering for our sin, so that we could be made right with God through Christ." Those who follow Jesus follow a Savior who truly paid the ultimate price so that we could have eternal life with Him. Jesus gave His life as an atoning sacrifice (propitiation) for our sins.

PRACTICAL APPLICATION:

The best gift you've ever received
What was the best gift you ever received as an elementary school-aged child? A new bike? A family vacation to Walt Disney World? A surprise birthday party? A toy or gadget you had been hoping to receive for a long time? It would be enjoyable to hear what comes to your mind when you remember one of the greatest gifts you ever received as a young child.

How about as a teenager? What was a really memorable gift you received? A newly remodeled room (decorated specifically to your own design)? A love note from the boy or girl you were certain would be "the one?" The keys to the most beautiful clunker-of-a-car that you could now call your very own? I am sure that if we had time, we would all have a good laugh over the things that we once valued so deeply.

Now, how about as an adult? What was a really memorable gift you received in recent years? An original gift from one of your children involving dried macaroni noodles, colored yarn, and a triple-tied knot that barely slipped over your head so you could proudly wear your new necklace? An award, an encouraging letter, or an acknowledgement of your significant contribution at your workplace, church or community gathering? Your appreciation of your spouse taking care of chores around the house, which allows you to enjoy the gift of "free-time" to do whatever you choose to do? It is amazing how our "greatest gifts" list changes over time.

Who gave it to you?
Now return to these questions and recall, "WHO" gave you these gifts? For some, I bet it was a parent, grandparent, loved one, spouse, or a dear friend who gave you these gifts. In fact, I wonder if in the above scenarios you

would say that it was the gift itself that made it "great," or if it really was the "giver" of the gift that made it extra special and memorable?

Was this on your list?
Now for the final question: In any of your above lists of memorable gifts, did you make reference to anyone who "took your punishment for something you deserved" as one of the best gifts you had ever received in life? Every believer in Jesus Christ is the recipient of this greatest gift of all—having Jesus Christ, the sinless One, pay for the punishment of our sin by suffering a horrific death upon a cross. The more we think about what our lives would have been without being pardoned and at peace with God (i.e., propitiation), the more the believer is grateful for such an undeserving gift from God.

See how it feels
There is one very practical way to remain appreciative of Jesus Christ's payment for our sins—to see how it feels. I am not suggesting that you literally take the blame for co-workers or friends. But one very practical way to remain mindful of how great Jesus' gift of salvation was to us is to pretend that you have offered to take the blame for someone else's mistakes. It won't take you more than a couple times pretending before you will begin to feel how much pain and suffering you would experience. Just imagine what would happen if you interrupted a real scenario and said, "Excuse me. This is all my fault. Blame me, not them!" Your heart would scream within you, "Wait, my life has now been majorly inconvenienced . . . it's not fair . . . I don't deserve this . . . this is nonsense . . . they can fend for themselves . . ." For example, if at night you drive by a police officer who has pulled a car over, and just as open bottles of alcohol are found, you stop and say, "Excuse me officer. This is my car and this is all my fault." The police officer believes you and lets the real offender go. You are a law-abiding citizen and you are taken into custody to pay for someone else's crime. Now in another scenario, imagine what your social life would be like if you agreed to accept every detention hour of your former high school classmates. Or, consider how you would feel if you were imprisoned for life for a crime you didn't commit, but you willingly accepted the sentence of incarceration for another person you never even met. Furthermore, that person for whom you took the punishment never came to visit you or to thank you. And, worse yet, that person cursed your name openly and unapologetically for being an unloving person.

If you are like me, you probably would stop pretending at this point—the feelings are too profound and the thoughts are too disturbing. But if you really take this scenario to heart, you can get a glimpse of how much love it took Jesus Christ to willingly take upon Himself the payment for your sin. It also shows how much unparalleled love the God of the Universe has for you.

Read on

I encourage you to immediately read the chapter on "Conversion" and learn how you can respond to such a great gift that Jesus Christ provided for you and me! It will bring the above scenario to an amazingly merciful conclusion and provide a portrait of God's great compassion that still continues for you today.

Consider studying more Bible verses that refer to the concept of propitiation

Here are some more verses to read on this topic—1 John 2:2; Romans 3:25-26; Leviticus 4:15; Hebrews 2:17.

Write it down... →

...& make it
HAPPEN!

TWENTY FIVE

CONVERSION

(KUHN-VUR-ZHUHN)

"Our willing response to the gospel call, in which we sincerely repent of sins and place our trust in Christ for salvation."
- WAYNE GRUDEM, Bible Doctrine, 481

The Greek word commonly used for salvation is the word, sōtēria, which
means "deliverance" or "salvation." There are many theological terms associated with the concept of salvation, including words like regeneration,
conversion and sanctification. A very helpful overview is presented in the
following definition in the Pocket Dictionary of Theological Terms under
conversion :

> "A GENERAL TERM REFERRING TO AN INDIVIDUAL'S INITIAL ENCOUNTER with God
> in Christ resulting in the reception of God's gracious provision
> of salvation. Some of the changes brought about in conversion
> include a change in heart from being dead in sin to being alive in
> Christ (regeneration, John 1:12-13), a change in status from be-
> ing guilty before God to being not guilty (justification, Romans
> 3:21-31), a change in relationship from being an outcast and enemy
> to being a child and friend of God (adoption and reconciliation, 1
> John 3:1; Colossians 1:20). Conversion begins the journey of dis-
> cipleship through which a person who once was a slave to sin is
> being freed by the Holy Spirit for holiness (sanctification)" (30).

Since the concepts of regeneration and sanctification are addressed elsewhere in this book, the focus of this entry will be on conversion. There are
four considerations to address connected with the concept of conversion:

Conversion includes the entire person
The entire person includes an individual's intellect, emotions and will.
When it comes to matters of salvation and conversion, the entire person
is involved in the process. Conversion is not just an intellectual decision, as
though we reason our way to God. It is not just an emotional decision, as
though we feel sorrow and remorse and are therefore saved. It is not just a
choice that we make to follow Jesus. Salvation includes all of these components—through the work of Jesus and the new life provided by the Holy
Spirit.

Repentance is more than just feeling sorry
In 2 Corinthians 7:10 the apostle Paul speaks of a godly repentance and a
worldly sorrow. The Greek word used in the passage is metanoia, and it is

to be understood as "a change of mind." Many people feel sorry about sin. They may feel bad that they hurt someone else, or they may feel bad that they were caught doing something wrong, but that feeling of remorse is not what metanoia means. The idea of "a change of mind" suggests going in a different direction—actively turning from sin and turning to God.

Faith is a gift from God
Faith is a gift from God, and it is a not a result of the works that we have done (Ephesians 2:8-10). The biblical concept of faith is seen many places in the Bible, and it should be remembered that God provides us with the faith to believe in Him. The Greek word is pistis, which means to have a conviction about the truth of something.

Fruit is a result of salvation, not its cause
In James 3 we are instructed that faith without works is dead. It is important to keep in mind that James is speaking about works after salvation, not works leading to salvation. Many religions of the world teach that in order to obtain salvation, the individual must do something; that you and I must earn our place in heaven. The Bible communicates a much different story. The Bible teaches that in order to be saved, we cannot rely on ourselves, but we must offer ourselves entirely to God. The Bible teaches that only God can bring about salvation in our lives. The apostle Paul makes this very clear in his statements about salvation in the book of Romans, especially in Romans 3:28, "So we are made right with God through faith and not by obeying the law."

PRACTICAL APPLICATION:

It is difficult to think of any other concept more important for every human being to comprehend than their need to be forgiven from their sins and their soul saved from the penalty of their sinfulness by the Lord Jesus Christ. Some people come to this realization very early in life. Some people ask God to save them from their sinfulness moments before they take their last breath. Still others take a fair amount of time grappling with the teachings of the Bible until they ultimately surrender their will to God and ask Him to forgive them of their sin and save their souls. And, unfortunately, there are some who never accept Jesus Christ as the only One who is able to offer forgiveness of their sin. And still there are those among this latter group who never even come to the acknowledgement that their souls are in need of saving.

I wonder where you are in this above list of people. Have you ever heard the message of your need for salvation but ignored it for some reason? Have you thought about the truth that all mankind needs to be saved by God? Or do you choose to ignore that reality by diverting your attention to something else in order not to think about it? Are you avoiding making a decision to accept Jesus Christ as your personal Savior? Have you en-grossed yourself in activities, work and social activities so as not to have to think about the repercussions of choosing to reject Jesus Christ? Are you currently grappling with spiritual discussions? Or have you looked back on how long you've said you would consider these things, and now you real-ize that it has been years? And, quite honestly, you have never determined when you will finally make your decision . . . or you never plan on making a decision! Have you been disappointed by someone's words and/or actions who claimed to be a "Christian?" Are you still pointing to that person's horrible testimony as "Exhibit A"—and that's why you have not placed your own faith in Jesus Christ? It's sad but true, sometimes Christians fail miser-ably, but their failure is totally irrelevant to your own decision to accept Christ. Maybe you haven't really experienced a spiritual battle within your soul. Maybe you're kind, gracious and professionally accomplished. You would say that you basically are living a "good" life, but you haven't really engaged the spiritual question of salvation. Have you focused on living a commendable life today rather than taking time to appraise what your life will be like for eternity? Or maybe the story of your life is even more diverse than these scenarios. Regardless of your personal life situation, one thing is clear according to the Bible—every individual must make a personal deci-sion as to their spiritual life.

" HAVE YOU FOCUSED ON LIVING A COMMEND-ABLE LIFE TODAY RATHER THAN TAKING TIME TO APPRAISE WHAT YOUR LIFE WILL BE LIKE FOR ETERNITY? "

A necessary rehearsal of God's gift of salvation that is available to you
Where ever you are in your life's journey, I encourage you to take a moment to consider the truth of how you can know that you can have peace with God:

1. Romans 3:23 teaches that every human being is spiritually "lost!"
Because we have fallen short (or "don't measure up") to God's holi-ness . . . and we all have sin in our hearts . . . and we are all going to be punished for that sin . . . and there is NOTHING WE HUMANLY CAN DO ABOUT IT . . . then, we're hopelessly lost! And in order to be "saved," you first have to come to the realization that you are lost.

2. Romans 6:23 teaches that every person has "merited" or "de-serves" God's punishment for that sin.
Because God is holy (i.e., perfect/sinless), He must punish sin—no ques-tion. God can never "wink" at sin or let it go past Him. God has to—and

will—punish sin.

3. Ephesians 2:8-9 and Titus 3:5 teach that we can't save ourselves in any possible way.
And if this were the end of the story, there would be NO hope, NO peace, NO comfort, NO joy, and NO salvation available to you and me. But fortunately, God extends His own offer for us to accept His free gift of salvation!

4. Romans 5:8 assures us that all hope is not lost!
It IS possible to have peace with God!

5. Romans 10:9-10 summarizes what we need to believe in order to receive God's salvation:
(1) Agree with God about your sinful state; (2) Believe that Jesus is God!; (3) Believe that Jesus' sacrifice was sufficient to pay for your sins; (4) Believe that Jesus physically rose from the dead—proving that He can conquer both physical and spiritual death; (5) Place your trust in His promise to save you!

I encourage you to ask God to forgive you from your sin and to save your soul today
Simply pray (i.e., just talk) to God and affirm with Him that you accept all that the Bible says about salvation (above). Then, spend a moment thanking Him for saving your soul today! After which, I encourage you to tell another Christian of your decision so that you have another person to walk this spiritual journey with you. And read on throughout the remainder of this book to learn how the Bible can practically affect your life today.

Study what the Bible says about the need to experience salvation in your own life
Here are some more verses to read on this topic—Hebrews 11; Acts 9:1-30; Acts 4:12; John 10:1-21; Ephesians 2:8-10.

Write it down... ⟶

...& make it
HAPPEN!

THE CHURCH

BAPTISM

(BAP-TIZ-UHM)

"The view that baptism is appropriately administered only to those who give a believable profession of faith in Jesus Christ."
- WAYNE GRUDEM, Bible Doctrine, 480

#1

The word baptism is the Greek word, baptisma, which means "immersion" or "submersion." It is a doctrine that is foundational to a Christian's belief system, and yet it is a doctrine that has been debated within Evangelical communities for hundreds of years. The practice itself is clearly evidenced within the pages of Scripture, as even Jesus is recorded as having been baptized by John the Baptist (see Matthew 3 and Luke 3). The Bible speaks of the physical act of baptizing individuals, but it also speaks of the spiritual significance of baptism. Furthermore, baptism is used symbolically within Scripture. Consider Romans 6:4 which states, "For we died and were buried with Christ by baptism. And just as Christ was raised from the dead by the glorious power of the Father, now we also may live new lives." It is the Christian's co-crucifixion and co-resurrection with Christ that is proclaimed every time a believer is baptized.

#2

The examples in the New Testament of believers professing faith in the risen Jesus are followed by that individual being baptized. Consider the story of Philip and the Ethiopian traveler in Acts 8. In this story Philip explains Isaiah 53 to the Ethiopian, and the man professes faith in Jesus. Afterwards the Ethiopian is recorded as saying, "Look! There's some water! Why can't I be baptized" (Acts 8:36)? The story in Acts 10 records another conversion experience about the Roman centurion, Cornelius. After their profession of faith in the risen Jesus, all of these individuals were baptized.

You may be wondering why there is a controversy about baptism if it is so clearly taught within the Bible. The challenges come not with the fact of the teaching, but more with the implementation and significance of the act itself. Some suggest that individuals are saved because of the act of baptism. These would indicate that without baptism, an individual cannot be saved. Others would suggest the way in which someone is baptized does not have significance. This leads some to practice what is known as "sprinkling" with water, or "pouring" water on the head of an individual instead of immersion. Still others believe that infants should be baptized as a sign of their participation in the Kingdom of God.

With all of this in mind, let us take a quick look at what Scripture says about baptism. It seems that Scripture presents baptism as being an outward display of an inward reality. It is commanded by Jesus (Matthew 28:19) and the apostles (Acts 2:38). As Wayne Grudem suggests, "To say that baptism or any other action is necessary for salvation is to say that we are not justified by faith alone, but by faith plus a certain 'work,' the work of baptism" (384). In discussing the various aspects of conversion and justification, it is evident from Scripture that an individual is justified (declared righteous) not because of anything they do, but through the work of Jesus. Baptism is to be viewed as an act of obedience and an act of identifying with the assembly of believers, but not as something which actually saves the individual.

PRACTICAL APPLICATION:

Back to school
I don't know what it is about Kindergarten, but the Kindergarten year seems to be one of the most memorable years out of all the school years. Maybe it is because of all the "firsts" that come with the first official year of school—first time away from the family for an entire day (or half a day), first time meeting new people who live beyond "next door" or down the street, first lunch box that you can arrange and rearrange exactly like you want it, first time struggling with the temptation of "should I tell . . . or should I not tell Mom that I traded that gross tuna and pickle sandwich with a classmate for his bag of sour cream and onion potato chips and a candy bar (. . . don't ask me how I came up with these particular menu choices—what happens in Kindergarten, stays in Kindergarten)!

But probably the number one reason why Kindergarten has made an indelible mark in many of our minds is the fact that for the first time we were now responsible to present our own thoughts and feelings to other people without having someone else speak for us. We were given the opportunity to talk to our adult teacher all by ourselves, negotiate with newly found friends one-on-one and discover a wonderful thing called independence.

"Show and Tell"
And there was the event where we were able to utilize all of these newly found skills into one experience—"Show and Tell!" It was the time we could choose our own item from home, take it to school and present it exactly how we felt it should be described. With no scrutiny from parents, we were able to express our feelings about it and the story behind it. And afterwards, we were all commended for our excellent job and encouraged to keep up the good work.

I liken baptism to "show and tell." In baptism, you are telling a watching world in your own unique way about the change that God has already made in your life. For what God did in the quietness of your heart is now being proclaimed to everyone, so they can hear your story and understand why you are getting baptized.

> **" IN BAPTISM, YOU ARE TELLING A WATCH-ING WORLD IN YOUR OWN UNIQUE WAY ABOUT THE CHANGE THAT GOD HAS ALREADY MADE IN YOUR LIFE. "**

Here are some practical ways in which the concept of "baptism" can affect your actions today:

1. Celebrate the newcomers
Angels rejoice when one sinner has been forgiven of their sins and saved by Jesus Christ; so, shouldn't we get equally excited? Luke 15:10 says, "There is joy in the presence of God's angels when even one sinner repents." In many big churches today, we often don't learn of someone having accepted Christ as their personal Savior until many days later—when they get baptized. So when someone gets bap-tized, it ought to be considered a big celebration! Don't withhold your excitement for one who has chosen to tell the world of their changed life through Jesus Christ! Throw a party for them. Encourage them to come to your house and share their story of life-change with other friends and family. Make sure your children watch your friend's baptism, so you can give them that all-powerful visual of how your friend told the world that they now are a child of God!

2. Ask others to describe their baptism moment with you
Find out when it occurred, where they were baptized and how long they waited to be baptized after they accepted Christ as their per-sonal Savior. If there was a delay between putting their faith in Jesus Christ and being baptized, ask them the reason for the delay. Was it because they were afraid of the water? Did they have unsaved family members who did not want them to be baptized? Did they not know the importance of being baptized as a new believer in Jesus Christ? By asking people these and other questions, you may learn some common objections that will help you in the future when you discuss the subject of baptism.

3. Consider being baptized yourself
In just a few minutes of researching this topic, you will learn that baptism was a process of initiation and an announcement into a belief system. You'll learn how there were different types of "baptisms" even in non-Christian religions. Some used water and some used different

ways to baptize. So, even though the concept of baptism was not original with Christianity, the statement that baptism makes about a person is profound. Have you accepted Jesus Christ as your personal Savior? If so, have you been baptized in order to publicly announce your decision to put your faith in Jesus Christ? Ask a pastor, professor, or Christian friend to point you in the right direction.

Study what the Bible says about baptism
Here are some more verses to read on this topic—Romans 6; Matthew 3:13-17; Mark 1:9-11; Luke 3:21-23.

Write it down... →

...& make it HAPPEN!

LORD'S SUPPER/COMMUNION

(KUH-MYOON-YUHN)

> "As they were eating, Jesus took some bread and blessed it.
> Then he broke it in pieces and gave it to the disciples, saying,
> 'Take this and eat it, for this is my body.' And he took a cup
> of wine and gave thanks to God for it. He gave it to them and
> said, 'Each of you drink from it, for this is my blood, which con-
> firms the covenant between God and his people. It is poured
> out as a sacrifice to forgive the sins of many."
> - MATTHEW 26:26-28

Just hours before His arrest, trials and crucifixion, Jesus shared His last meal with His disciples. The meal that Jesus shared with His disciples carried much significance in both an Old Testament context and a New Testament context. The meal they shared was called the Passover, which is a meal of remembrance of the Lord's deliverance of His people (Israel) from the Egyptians (see Exodus 11 and 12). Devout Jews were to celebrate the Passover in accordance with the Old Testament regulations (Deuter-onomy 16:1-8). It was this Passover meal that Jesus commemorated with His disciples. However, the meal took on a greater significance with Jesus' words when He said that the bread was His body, and that the wine was His blood.

Although there is at times much debate over the exact meaning of Jesus' words, it seems clear from the text that Jesus was using the bread and the wine as symbolic representations of His sacrifice for the sins of the world. Just as the Passover lamb was a sacrifice without defect or blemish, so Jesus was to be offered as the perfect sacrifice for the sins of the world. Je-sus wanted to make sure His followers would always remember the signifi-cance of His work on the cross.

The apostle Paul considers the importance of the Lord's Supper when he challenges his readers to participate in this remembrance—but only if they have first examined themselves to make sure they participate with pure motives (see 1 Corinthians 11). He even mentions that some within the church were sick and some had even died, due to their indifferent attitude when participating in the Lord's Supper.

The Lord's Supper is considered one of two ordinances within many Chris-tian churches (baptism being the other ordinance). Both of these ordinanc-es carry symbolic significance for believers. A person does not become saved by keeping the Lord's Supper, just as a person does not become saved by being baptized. But both ordinances are steps of obedience to Jesus' commands, and both are done to commemorate the work of Jesus.

R.S. Wallace illustrates the significance of the Lord's Supper in his explanation in the Evangelical Dictionary of Theology. In the entry on the Lord's Supper he states the following: "There is in the Lord's Supper a constant renewal of the covenant between God and the church. The word "remembrance" (anamnesis) refers not simply to man's remembering of the Lord, but also to God's remembrance of His Messiah and His covenant and of His promise to restore the kingdom. At the supper all this is brought before God in true intercessory prayer" (705). Jesus is truly blessed when His people remember His death, burial and resurrection through their observance of the Lord's Supper.

PRACTICAL APPLICATION:

Stacking up the memorabilia

Whenever I travel, I make it a habit to buy one or two trinkets to place on the bookshelf in my office. Those trinkets are wonderful reminders of my various trips. Even today as I look at them I remember details of each trip— the length of the trip, the emotions I felt while I was there, and the unique scenery of each destination. For example, I have a mug from a coffee shop in Israel. I have a ticket stub that gave me access to the Empire State Building in New York City. I have a little hacky sack (a small, round bean-bag) from one of the country pavilions in Walt Disney World's Epcot theme park. I have a candid picture of my children holding hands while walking in front of me at a favorite vacation spot. Each piece of memorabilia reminds me of the experience and the meaning of different trips.

While at work, I often find myself looking at my memorabilia. It tends to relax me, and the memories cause me to smile—even to regain a balance in my personal life. My collection reminds me that work is a vitally important part of life, and that it is honorable to put in a good and hard day's work. It is just as important to work hard on making sure that my family life is equally as important. As a result, I often tell my students that I'm okay if they get a "C" in their class as long as they make sure they retain an "A" in their family life. It is good to remember that there is more to life than just the current moment.

Don't forget to remember

The night before Jesus was to be crucified upon a cross, He had a final dinner with His closest friends. He turned to them and reminded them of the sacrifice that He was about to make on their behalf. During the previous three years with these close friends, Jesus had promised that He would rise from the dead. So on this somber evening, He made a point to remind them once again that He would not only suffer, but He would rise again. He then referenced His ultimate return back to earth, which would require Him to first leave the earth after His resurrection. Even if the details of the conversation became blurred in His friends' minds, one thing was certain; there was yet more to come in God's calendar of events after the crucifixion of Jesus Christ.

> **I'M OKAY IF THEY GET A 'C' IN THEIR CLASS AS LONG AS THEY MAKE SURE THEY RETAIN AN 'A' IN THEIR FAMILY LIFE. IT IS GOOD TO REMEMBER THAT THERE IS MORE TO LIFE THAN JUST THE CURRENT MOMENT.**

Knowing that what Jesus was about to do would change the world forever, He commanded His friends to regularly perform an action that would cause them to remember the importance of His sacrifice on the cross. Jesus requires all believers in Jesus Christ—from the first ones to believers today—to regularly engage in the ordinance of Communion (sometimes referred to as the "Lord's Supper"). He wanted them (and us) to remember that moment He had with His disciples in the Upper Room and the sacrifice He made on the cross (1 Corinthians 11:24-26).

Note to self
It is incumbent upon all believers not only to remember, but also to appreciate the goodness of God in their lives. If you are a believer in Jesus Christ, I encourage you to make it a priority to participate in Communion every time your church takes time to remember the Lord in this fashion. I encourage you to take that time to perform some spiritual reflection and thank God for saving your soul, guiding you throughout your life through His Word, and for the very reality of being able to have a personal relationship with Him—the God of the Universe.

In addition, I encourage you to vividly remember specific moments in your life that God either taught you an indelible life-lesson, opened your eyes to His truth in a specific situation or how He affected your thinking in a way you never imagined, etc. It may involve you writing in a journal or in the cover of your Bible about the miracles you have experienced. It might be helpful to write out what you would like to pray to God. Then, retain a copy of that note in a secure place in order to recall with perfect clarity exactly what you pleaded for to God—and how He specifically responded to you in that situation. You should keep in mind, however, that while these writings and memorabilia will be precious artifacts to you, they are only artifacts. And while you will certainly revisit these items in the days to come, be sure to remember that it is not the ceremony or practice of writing things down that delivers you from your troubles, but rather the personal God to Whom you are writing that provides peace and comfort in your life.

Study what the Bible says about the Lord's Supper/Communion
Here are some more verses to read on this topic—Matthew 26:26-30; Mark 14:22-26; Luke 22:14-20; 1 Corinthians 11:23-26.

Write it down... ↘

...& make it
HAPPEN!

ECCLESIA/THE CHURCH

(IH-KLEE-ZHEE-UH)

"Instead, we will speak the truth in love, growing in every way more and more like Christ, who is the head of his body, the church. He makes the whole body fit together perfectly. As each part does its own special work, it helps the other parts grow, so that the whole body is healthy and growing and full of love."
- EPHESIANS 4:15-16

The church exists to equip followers of Christ (Ephesians 4:11-12). The one, true universal church is made up of believers from all walks of life, from all backgrounds and from various denominational affiliations. The Greek term is ekklēsia, meaning "called out ones" or the "assembly." Originally the word was applied to a gathering of people, but in Matthew 16:18, Jesus said that He will build His church; He will build His kind of assembly. The church is not a building, the church is not a pastor, and the church is not great music programs. The church is the assembly. The church is the people.

The first church recorded in the New Testament did not have a building or a specific program to follow, but they did have each other, and they were committed to gathering together. But why did they gather together, and what was the significance of that gathering? We get a glimpse of what happened in the church from reading the book of Acts. It describes what was happening during the early days of the church. One of the key passages to consider is found in Acts 2:42, "All the believers devoted themselves to the apostles' teaching, and to fellowship, and to sharing in meals (including the Lord's Supper), and to prayer." A few key elements are seen in this verse of Scripture, and it has been used for many different books and sermons, but there is a relevant point for our purposes. Notice the first three words of the verse, "All the believers. . . . "

There is an ongoing conversation about the make-up of the assembly. Who are those individuals that make up the assembly of God? From this text and others throughout the New Testament, it seems clear that the church is a group of believers. The purpose, then, is for this assembly of believers to gather together and to devote themselves to the work of God, for the glory of God. Combine this understanding of the church as a group of believers with what we read in Ephesians 4:11-12. That passage indicates that God has given "the church: the apostles, the prophets, the evangelists, and the pastors and teachers. Their responsibility is to equip God's people to do his work and build up the church, the body of Christ." Did you notice the reason God gave the apostles, prophets, evangelists and pastor/teachers? It is to equip the saints for the work of the ministry.

Too often we have a mindset that the church leadership—the pastor, the youth pastor, the music director—should be ministering to an unsaved world. But in reality, we (those of us who are non-church-staff people) should be the ones doing the work of the ministry. It is the responsibility of the church leadership to help equip you and me to carry out the mission of God here on the earth.

The church should come alongside the individual and help build him or her up and encourage that person in his or her faith, but the important thing to keep in mind is that the church is made up of individuals. If you are burdened thinking that the church should do this or that, then it is very likely that God is wanting you to lead fellow believers in that ministry. The church is not corporately more than what we are individually. I do not mean by that statement that corporately we cannot do more than we can as individuals. Rather, we cannot expect those in leadership (often seen as "the church") to do something that we are not willing to do as individuals (those of us who make up the majority of "the church").

PRACTICAL APPLICATION:

"Who's on first?"
Early in the twentieth century, the comedy duo Abbott and Costello made famous the play-on-words sketch entitled, "Who's on first." Applying words like "Who" and "What" and "Which" for people's names in their fictional story makes for a humorous conversation when they attempt to talk about specific individuals. The story gets convoluted because the names of the people ("Who" or "What" or "Which") are used in multiple ways in the dialogue. When the simple question is asked, "Who's on first?" The answer comes back, "Who is on first" (the player's name is "Who"). "That's what I'm asking, 'Who is on first?'" "You're right. He is." The more they talk the more the confusion builds. At the end of the dialogue Abbott and Costello are exacerbated with each other, and the audience is left laughing about the entire scene.

"Who's the 'church'?"
I have occasionally found that the same level of confusion occurs when people today attempt to discuss the concept of "the church." When I ask people "who is the church?" I receive many different responses. "It is that building over there . . . and over there . . . and around the corner." Or some say there are only specific denominations that represent the true church, and so on. According to the Bible, the "church" is a title placed upon a person who has accepted Jesus Christ as his/her personal Savior (see the chapter on "Salvation"). Immediately upon salvation, that person is a part

of God's "church."

Tear down the walls
When God looks down upon the world, He sees two types of people—people who have placed their faith in Jesus Christ and have received forgiveness of their sin; and people who have not placed their faith in Jesus Christ and have not received forgiveness of their sin. Those who have accepted Jesus as their Savior are members of "the church" (i.e., the "family of God," "children of God," or the "household of faith" according to Galatians 6:10). And those who have not accepted Jesus as their Savior are not members of His family. Remember, we all are God's creations, but we are not all God's children—not until we have put our faith in Jesus Christ as our Savior (again, see the chapter on "Salvation").

So, when you look at a church building on the corner of your street, imagine the walls disappearing and being able to see right inside the souls of every person that is attending that church service. Everyone that has accepted Christ as their Savior is a member of God's true church. And everyone who has not accepted Christ is not a member of God's true church—even though they are standing directly inside of a church building!

Here is how the reality of God's true church can affect you practically today:

1. Grow the family
Our goal should be to grow the family of God. So, share with others how they can be a part of the family of God.

> " YOU SHOULD ENJOY THOSE TIMES WHEN THE "FAMILY OF GOD" FILLS IN THE GAPS THAT YOUR OWN PHYSICAL FAMILIES HAVE NOT (OR COULD NOT) PROVIDE FOR YOU. "

2. Love your new family
If you have accepted Christ as your Savior, you have been adopted into a second family! A family that is expected to reflect the love that your heavenly Father has for you—unconditional, pure from sin and eternal love. God takes this "family" relationship very seriously. You should too. You should enjoy those times when the "family of God" fills in the gaps that your own physical families have not (or could not) provide for you. It shouldn't be surprising that the Bible uses many familial analogies when talking about believers relating to each other: "Therefore, whenever we have the opportunity, we should do good to everyone—

especially to those in the family of faith" (Galatians 6:10). "No, I will not abandon you as orphans—I will come to you" (John 14:18). "God decided in advance to adopt us into his own family by bringing us to himself through Jesus Christ. This is what he wanted to do, and it gave him great pleasure" (Ephesians 1:5). "So now you Gentiles are no longer strangers and foreigners. You are citizens along with all of God's holy people. You are members of God's family" (Ephesians 2:19). "Those who have been born into God's family do not make a practice of sinning, because God's life is in them" (1 John 3:9a).

3. Intentionally engage your spiritual family
Hebrews 10:25 encourages us not to "forsake" or "avoid" or "ignore" the fellowship of our spiritual family as it can provide a level of edification and encouragement that nothing else can. "And let us not neglect our meeting together, as some people do, but encourage one another. . . " (Hebrews 10:25).

4. Find a local assembly of believers and enjoy the family
Just as you were encouraged when the topic of "church membership" was discussed, find a local assembly of believers with whom to "do life." Just as our physical families are in our lives 24/7, the family of God is a source of encouragement, accountability and edification that should be an ingredient in any spiritually mature person's life all week long as well—not just on Sundays.

Study what the Bible says about the biblical meaning of ecclesia (church)
Here are some more verses to read on this topic—Ephesians 4:7-16; Acts 2:40-47; 1 Corinthians 12:12; Revelation 19:8; Ephesians 5:22-32.

Write it down... ⟶

...& make it
HAPPEN!

"An elder is a manager of God's household, so he must live a blameless life. He must not be arrogant or quick-tempered; he must not be a heavy drinker, violent, or dishonest with money. Rather, he must enjoy having guests in his home, and he must love what is good. He must live wisely and be just. He must live a devout and disciplined life. He must have a strong belief in the trustworthy message he was taught; then he will be able to encourage others with wholesome teaching and show those who oppose it where they are wrong."
- TITUS 1:7-9

There is much controversy surrounding the authority within a local congregation. The question is not typically about the authority that Jesus has over the church, as is evidenced in Ephesians 5:23 where it states that Christ is the head of the church. However, the issue of authority within the church does become more complicated when the matter of pastoral authority comes into play. Some denominational backgrounds affirm that the authority within the church rests within a single individual. These churches are said to have an Episcopal form of church government, and they use examples such as the apostle Paul to build their case for a single bishop or church leader (see Titus 1:5 and Acts 14:23).

Other churches claim that after the authority of Jesus, the authority within local congregations rests in a group of leaders (often called elders). This is a representative form of church government and is known as a Presbyterian model of church. Examples of this representative church are cited in Thessalonians 5:12-13 and Hebrews 13:17. Still other churches reject the idea of a single person (bishop) holding authority, and they also reject the idea of a group of leaders (elders) holding authority within the church. This third group of churches is said to be congregationally led in their practices. It is based on the understanding of the priesthood of all believers (see 1 Peter 2:9 and Acts 15:22).

With all of the controversy and disagreement surrounding the authority within the church, there are a few areas that the universal church of Jesus should seek to remember as they interact with one another:

Jesus is the head of the church
This point was already made, but it bears repeating. Jesus is the ultimate head of the church, and although you and I could disagree with where the

authority lies at the individual church level, we should be able to agree that ultimately Jesus is to be looked to as the authority in the church.

Accountability is important to the functioning of the body of Christ

It is important to keep in mind that any local congregation should have systems of accountability. This relates to the congregationally-led churches as well as elder-led churches—the leaders need to make sure they are being faithful to the words of Jesus found in the pages of Scripture. And it also applies to the bishop-led church where one person is structurally in charge of the rest of the church. In any of the three options, those in leadership need to be held accountable for their actions.

The mission of the church is to equip the saints to proclaim the gospel to the world #9

At first this may seem to be off topic, but in reality, it is vitally important that the purpose of the church (the assembly of believers) be kept in focus when talking about church leadership and authority. There is a vulnerability of any church, and any church government, to become so wrapped up in some details that the church corporately forgets why they exist as a local congregation in the first place. The church is to be equipping the saints for the work of the ministry (Ephesians 4), and as individuals we have a tremendous responsibility to share the gospel with the world around us (Matthew 28:18-20).

PRACTICAL APPLICATION:

Not for the faint of heart

There is a segment of the community of believers who bear a heavier load of responsibility than other believers—church leaders. James cautions all believers in the church that they should not rush to sign up for a leadership position without giving it careful thought and prayer. The reason being, church leaders' actions will be scrutinized much more severely than the actions of those who do not hold a leadership position within the church. James 3:1 says, "Dear brothers and sisters, not many of you should become teachers in the church, for we who teach will be judged more strictly." In Acts 6:3b, Luke reminds us that the church leaders were chosen based upon being "well respected and full of the Spirit and wisdom. We will give them this responsibility." In 1 Timothy 3 and Titus 1, the apostle Paul reminds all leaders of the additional qualifications incumbent upon them.

God is not so much impressed with a leader's name plate on the door as much as He is concerned about their conduct and how they maintain their responsibility. So, even if the church leader volunteers his/her time and does not receive compensation for their work at the church, or whether or not they have a personal office at the church, or whether they participate in the church's regularly scheduled church service(s), every leader, to whatever degree, is responsible to lead the community of believers according to God's Word to the best of their ability.

Get to know your church leaders

Take time to engage your church leaders in conversation. Learn from others who know them. Ask others to testify to you of how your church leader has impacted their lives. By doing this, you step into their shoes and learn of not only those things that they've done for other people, but also how profound their commitment is to the spiritual health of the community of believers.

Pray for your church leaders

There is no greater gift to give your church leadership than offering prayers on their behalf. As a result of getting to know your church leaders, you will be able to more intelligently pray for each of them. The more you learn about all they do for the community of believers, the more you can ask God to give them strength for their days to come. You can pray for their spiritual vitality to study God's Word each day. You can pray for them to remain spiritually sensitive to the Holy Spirit in order to know exactly what God would have them say to the next fellow believer who comes to them for spiritual advice. You need to pray for them because this level of spiritual maturity does not come easy or naturally.

> " THERE IS NO GREATER GIFT TO GIVE YOUR CHURCH LEADERSHIP THAN OFFERING PRAYERS ON THEIR BEHALF. "

Honor your church leaders

God has appointed spiritual leaders in our life in order to provide us with human examples on how to obey God in our daily lives. It is a hard, challenging life to lead God's people, but He has called many to do it. Therefore, esteem them, encourage them and obey them just as long as they provide the church with a God-honoring example. Paul said the following of his own leadership in 1 Corinthians 11:1, "And you should imitate me, just as I imitate Christ." The key words are "as I imitate Christ." While it is true that even church leaders will make mistakes (they are humans too), even in resolving their own mistakes, they should have God's honor in mind as their priority. So, as long as your church leadership is following Christ, you should very happily and willingly follow their leadership.

Study what the Bible says about church leadership

Here are some more verses to read on this topic—1 Timothy 3:1-7; Titus 1: 5-16; Ephesians 4:11-16; John 21:15-17; 1 Peter 4:11.

Write it down... ↘

...& make it
HAPPEN!

CHURCH MEMBERSHIP

"Now I say to you that you are Peter (which means 'rock'), and
upon this rock I will build my church, and all the powers of
hell will not conquer it."
- MATTHEW 16:18

Is there a need to be committed to, and connected with, a local congregation? For many years I resisted the idea that I needed to pledge a commitment to a local church community. It is not that I was not committed to attending on Sunday morning, or even using my giftedness within that local congregation, but I had a hesitation to make a visible commitment to that local church. Looking back at that time in my life, there was an uneasiness which I felt about the church, and I believed that I was giving the church my stamp of approval if I joined there as a member. In a way I believe I was correct at the time not to join the church. There were enough questions in my mind about the methodology and theology of that particular church that I think I made the right decision. However, my family and I left that congregation on good terms, and officially joined (as members) another local congregation.

The evidence in the New Testament for membership within a local congregation is varied, but it is supported by the biblical text. Consider the following three aspects of church membership that are seen within the pages of the New Testament:

First, it is important to be a member of a church because it is an indication of your commitment level to that local congregation. By seeking church membership, you are making a visible commitment to a local church and in turn, that congregation makes a commitment to you. This is not the same as a marriage ceremony, but some of the same principles should apply. You are pledging to assist the other members of that particular congregation through the good and the bad times.

Second, church discipline can only be effectively administered if, and when, individuals are committed to and connected with a local congregation. This may seem counterintuitive, since we do not typically like discipline, but consider the fact that you and I both need others to speak truth into our lives. By joining a local church you are, in effect, telling that congregation that they have permission to speak truth into your life, to hold you accountable to the Christian life they espouse, and you also will be doing the same within their lives. Church discipline is evidenced within the New Testament, especially in the church at Corinth. In 1 Corinthians 5, the apostle Paul addresses an issue within the church at Corinth concerning a sexual sin of one of its members. In 2 Corinthians 2:5-11, Paul again addresses an issue related to church discipline. Although these are likely two different individuals receiving church discipline, they are both examples of holding individuals accountable for their actions within the local congregation.

Finally, you have been spiritually gifted in order to serve a local congregation of believers. The apostle Paul talks about unity among the people of God, even though they have diverse gifts. Passages like Romans 12 and 1 Corinthians 12 convey this message, and these texts also speak to the uniqueness of the followers of Jesus. Church membership should not be something that you enter into lightly, but it should be something to which you give great consideration. It is within the context of the local congregation that your gifts of service to the community of believers are exercised.

PRACTICAL APPLICATION:

What's in it for me?
I recently walked into a fitness gym inquiring about membership. Before I even reached the front desk, I immediately noticed that to my left there was a long series of windows dividing the lobby from the main adult workout room. I stopped and admired the numerous machines—many of which I had no idea what they did for you, but they sure looked impressive! There were machines that seemed to focus on every specific muscle in your body. In fact, some worked on muscle groups I had no idea existed! My eyes blurred as I came across words that I don't usually use on a daily basis—words like triceps, biceps, deltoid, oblique, rotator, quads, lats, crunch, circuit, deadlift, dip belt, etc. Everywhere there were signs talking about things I had never considered before like body mass index, carb-watch and personal trainers. And of course to appeal to the novice (me!), there were plenty of posters for the purpose of motivating people to work out as they used phrases like, "Feel the burn." "Pain is weakness leaving the body!" "Like a walk in the park." And the ultimate poster was a photo of an extremely fit man pointing at you saying, "Ask about how a personal trainer can help you today!" You mean a guy like that will work side-by-side with me? Amazing.

What did it all mean? I didn't know but all I knew was that I wanted in! I wanted to take advantage of whatever those people on the other side of that glass were doing. I could not wait to get the most I could out of this workout facility.

All of this hype was strategically placed in plain view in order for me to experience the workout facility before I even made it to the front desk. So, it was no surprise that when I came to the front desk, my comment was not, "I'd like to get more information about membership." No, my question was, "What do I need to do to join today?" It was an easy decision because I saw firsthand all that I could take advantage of to better my physical life.

Unlike any other club

When people accept Jesus Christ as their personal Savior, they immediately become members in God's family, the church (see the chapter on " Ecclesia"). But being a member of God's church/family is a little different than joining a fitness club. When I joined the fitness club, I asked the question, "What's in it for me?" But when you are an active member of God's church, you are required to constantly ask, "What can I do for others?"

You see, when you join a local gathering of believers (i.e., a local church), you should immediately approach your membership as an avenue to share your abilities, passions and strengths with each other in order to edify others. Unfortunately, too many people search for a church looking for what it could provide them rather than asking how they could most serve in that particular body of believers. Remember that God equips you in order to be the best servant of Christ to others that you can possibly be. In 2 Timothy 2:2 this process is described in a clear and simple way, "You have heard me teach things that have been confirmed by many reliable witnesses. Now teach these truths to other trustworthy people who will be able to pass them on to others."

> **REMEMBER THAT GOD EQUIPS YOU IN ORDER TO BE THE BEST SERVANT OF CHRIST TO OTHERS THAT YOU CAN POSSIBLY BE.**

Here are a couple of spiritual questions to ask yourself about being an active member of the local church:

1. Are you a member of a biblically-focused local church?

After you have asked the vital questions regarding your own salvation (see the chapter on "Salvation"), it is critical to search out a congregation that creates an environment conducive for you to grow spiritually according to God's Word. Talk to people in the church. Engage the leadership and ask them if they too see the importance and priority of developing others spiritually according to what the Bible teaches. Then pray that God would direct you to a biblically-focused local church— the best one for you—to serve God and others.

2. Are you striving to be a "spiritual" personal trainer-in-training?

Are you looking for a more spiritually mature believer to assist you in becoming stronger in your faith? Have you considered becoming a spiritual trainer yourself? As long as you regularly spend time in God's Word, you will always have a word of encouragement or a biblical truth to share with others—regardless of how long you have been a Christian. James 5:16 describes how beneficial it can be to your fellow church members if you choose to consistently be "in-training." "Confess your sins to each other and pray for each other so that you may be healed. The earnest prayer of a righteous person has great power and produces wonderful results."

Study what the Bible says about participating in a local assembly of believers

Here are some more verses to read on this topic—Hebrews 10:25; Acts 2:40-47; 1 Corinthians 12:13-14; Ephesians 4:11-16.

Write it down... ↘

...& make it
HAPPEN!

THE CHRISTIAN LIFE

THE GREAT COMMANDMENT

(KUH-MAND-MUHNT)

> "'Teacher, which is the most important commandment in the
> law of Moses?' Jesus replied, 'You must love the LORD your
> God with all your heart, all your soul, and all your mind.' This
> is the first and greatest commandment. A second is equally
> important: 'Love your neighbor as yourself.' The entire law and
> all the demands of the prophets are based
> on these two commandments.'"
> - MATTHEW 22:36-40

The entire Old Testament requirements and demands can be summarized
with the words "love God and love others." Jesus' statement to the religious
leaders of His day challenged their understanding of what it means to really
be a follower of God. Jesus does not point to a single rule or command
from the Old Testament, but rather, He focuses right on the heart of the
matter—which is the heart of the individual. Jesus acknowledges that in order to truly obey the commands and requirements that God demands, the
individual's heart must be in the right place. The concept is seen throughout the Old Testament, especially in passages like Ezekiel 36, which speaks
of a new heart for the people of Israel. And also in Psalm 51, where David
acknowledges that God does not want empty sacrifices, but rather a heart
that is broken before Him (Psalm 51:16-19).

The words of Jesus in Matthew 22 should be understood to mean that as
individuals we are to love God with everything we have—"all your heart, all
your soul, and all your mind"—indicate our entire being. These words are
not to be understood as separate aspects of the person. In addition, the
word for love used in this passage is the Greek word, agapaō, which is one
of four Greek words used for love. This particular word is the most common
of the words for love used in the Bible, and it represents a self-sacrificing
and self-giving love. It is at times described as an unconditional love. Deuteronomy 6:5 communicates this idea using the Hebrew word, 'ahab,' which
means love. Deuteronomy 6 is also part of what is called the Shema, which
is a daily prayer of the people of Israel. This shows the closeness of this
message to the people's daily living.

As followers of Jesus, we are commanded by Him to love one another
(John 15:13), and we are not to love the world or the things of the world (1
John 2:15-17). We are to be committed to loving God and to loving one another. In John 13:35, Jesus says that the world will know us because of our
love for one another, which means that love should be a defining descrip

tion of the Christian community. Unfortunately, it seems that oftentimes the church is not known as a place of love. More often than we want to admit, followers of Jesus are known more for what they are opposed to, rather than for the love that should be characteristic in every believer's life.

PRACTICAL APPLICATION:

I hear what you're saying, but . . .
If I were pressed to identify the one most prominent reason people cite for why they are not Christians, it would be, "Christians don't live what they believe." I've also heard it said this way, "They preach 'love' but they don't demonstrate that love when they leave the church building." In my experience in dealing with college students, parishioners from many denominations, or people in the community, they all either know of someone or they themselves have turned away from listening to the message of Jesus Christ because they have been "burned" by so many Christians—Christians who have not displayed the level of love that Jesus Christ exhibited to others.

Burns can heal
I wish I could report that most people do a spiritual U-turn and begin to follow Jesus Christ as their Savior once they meet a spiritually loving and sincere Christian. Unfortunately, not all people do. It almost seems like it takes a number of good examples to engage the spiritually disgruntled person in order for them to overcome one negative example. This may not be the case for every person, but the good news is that individuals can recover from being "burned" by someone's poor example. In fact, regardless of how they were offended by a disobedient believer in the past, they have the responsibility to make the right decision about Jesus Christ and their need for salvation (see the chapter on "Salvation").

You can still jump over it
When dealing with those who have been offended by one who claims to be a Christian, go ahead and be honest with them. Agree that it is fair to admit that it is harder to accept the truths of Christianity after you've been treated poorly by a believer. Remind them that being a Christian doesn't mean we're claiming to be perfect. The truth is, there is no perfect human being walking on this earth! Let them know, in a respectful way, that someone else's lack of showing love is not a valid excuse to reject Jesus Christ. While it is true that someone has pushed the spiritual "high bar" much higher in their life, it is still not impossible to jump over. They can do it (and they must).

Put yourself out there
The best way to earn the trust of someone who has gotten burned is to offer yourself as an example to follow. I know this frightens many people as they immediately say, "What if I mess up?" Or, "What if I blow it one time—

they'll never listen to me again." The good news is that you don't have to try to be perfect in order to be a good example for an unbeliever to follow. The apostle Paul struck the right balance that all of us should adopt when serving as a spiritual example for someone to watch. He simply said, "And you should imitate me, just as I imitate Christ" (1 Corinthians 11:1).

Tell them that if they are looking for perfection, they should only look at Jesus Christ. Assure them that you will fail. But just as every marriage requires forgiveness and mercy in the relationship, likewise you would like to be trusted to make things right in the event you mess up. Remind them that even though you will probably mess up from time to time, you will always strive to obey God's way of making things right. And that even in the correction of missteps in your life, they will see that you are serious about following God in all things. The focus should be—when you obey Jesus, they can follow your example. And when you disobey Him, they are not to follow your example. In this way, they have to consciously assess your actions.

Accountability is good for you

While most people do not like to be "observed" for performance issues, it is healthy (and necessary) for the believer to be accountable to someone who is looking for advice and an example to follow. It occurs when children look up to parents. It is evident when students enroll in a professor's class. It even happens when relationships develop between two people. The point is, someone is always watching you—so let them see Christ! It will not only strengthen the onlooker, but it will also strengthen your own spiritual condition.

> " THE POINT IS, SOMEONE IS ALWAYS WATCHING YOU—SO LET THEM SEE CHRIST! "

Study what the Bible says about the Great Commandment

Here are some more verses to read on this topic—Matthew 22:34-40; Mark 12:28-34; John 3:16; 13:35.

Write it down... ↘

...& make it
HAPPEN!

THE GREAT COMMISSION

(KUH-MISH-UHN)

"Jesus came and told his disciples, 'I have been given all authority in heaven and on earth. Therefore, go and make disciples of all
the nations, baptizing them in the name of the Father and the Son
and the Holy Spirit. Teach these new disciples to obey all the commands I have given you. And be sure of this: I am with you
always, even to the end of the age.'"
- MATTHEW 28:18-20

The Great Commission is recorded five times in the Bible (Matthew 28:18-
20; Mark 16:15-18; Luke 24:44-48; John 20:19-23; Acts 1:3-8). It was included
as some of the last words Jesus shared with His disciples before His ascension. The Great Commission has become the focal point behind which
Christian churches rally. It is at the heart of what our focus should be as individual Christians. The Great Commission itself is centered on the concept
of making disciples.

The Greek word that is used for "disciples" is mathēteuō, meaning "to make
a disciple." It is important to keep in mind the significance of a disciple in
the first century Jewish mindset. With the idea of making a disciple comes
the process of teaching or instruction. This means that there is a strategic
communication of knowledge. Inherent to the Great Commission is the
message which the disciples are carrying. That message is the gospel (the
good news) of the death, burial and resurrection of Jesus (see 1 Corinthians
15:1-11).

Along with the idea of a disciple is also the concept of following someone.
When Jesus first called His disciples, He is recorded as saying, "Follow me."
Throughout His three years of ministry, the disciples learned more and
more what it meant to actually follow Jesus. They learned that to be the
greatest in the kingdom of God, they needed to become a servant of all
(Matthew 20:26), and that they must daily die to themselves, to their own
agenda (Luke 9:23-26).

To be a disciple means that Jesus is Lord of your life. In Romans 6 the apostle Paul speaks of the enslavement of sin within the life of those who do not
follow Jesus. Apart from the saving power of Jesus, the individual is a slave
to sin. But, Paul also talks about the victory over sin that followers of Jesus
can experience—"Sin is no longer your master" (Romans 6:14). However,
sometimes we neglect to read past verse 14. In the remainder of the chapter Paul argues that those who follow Jesus are now slaves to Jesus. In

committing your life to Jesus, you have made Jesus your Lord. As verse 18 records, "Now you are free from your slavery to sin, and you have become slaves to righteous living." But, think of the greatness of serving God in His kingdom. Think of the greatness of following Him, as you were designed by Him to live.

A final aspect of the Great Commission to think about is the idea that the Great Commission is to be extended to the whole world. In the first chapter of Acts we are instructed to start in Jerusalem, and eventually spread the good news throughout the entire world (Acts 1:8). As the Evangelical Dictionary of Theology states, "The method of carrying out the Great Commission involves preaching (2 Timothy 4:2) and teaching the Word (Matthew 28:20), with accompanying good works extended to all people (Acts 9:36; Galatians 6:9-10; Ephesians 2:10) for the glory of God" (1 Corinthians 10:31), (524).

PRACTICAL APPLICATION:

Great Commission-made-easy
If you are thinking to yourself, "There is no way I could talk to someone out in the community about spiritual things," you're not alone. But I believe that this fear can be diffused in most peoples' hearts if they actively engage in spiritual discussions among the ones with whom they feel comfortable. You see, fulfilling the Great Commission is not about having all the answers. When a question surfaces that you are unfamiliar with the answer, you can do research together. In fact, that research time actually helps to build trust between the Christian and the one inquiring about Christianity. The important first-step to fulfill the Great Commission is to engage a person in conversation regarding spiritual things. Fortunately, if you are accustomed to talking about spiritual things in your own circles, it will be much easier to engage in those conversations outside your circle of influence—especially if you do not hold yourself to the unrealistic expectations of always having to know all the answers. Even as a professor, I do not hold myself to that unrealistic expectation.

Ask questions . . . then ask more questions
Practice having intentional spiritual discussions with your family and/or friends—at a moment's notice about a variety of topics. Ask questions. Get the other person to do most of the talking so that you can begin to study the different perspectives people come from. Listen to people. Spend 80 percent of your initial conversation asking questions and taking mental notes on their level of spiritual understanding. Unfortunately, too many believers feel the need to dominate the conversation and to have all the answers when talking about spiritual things. But that doesn't have to be the case. You, as the believer, will learn more about the other person by asking questions and carefully listening to the answers that are given.

> **" PRACTICE HAVING INTENTIONAL SPIRITU-
> AL DISCUSSIONS WITH YOUR FAMILY AND/OR
> FRIENDS—AT A MOMENT'S NOTICE ABOUT A VA-
> RIETY OF TOPICS. "**

I've never been turned down
After every conversation with anyone—even unbelievers—I promise to pray for them that evening, and then I ask if I can say a quick prayer for them at that very moment. I have never been turned down by anyone. Sure, they hadn't anticipated the question, but they actually accept it as a very sincere and personal gesture that anyone would take that much interest in them personally. And when I pray, I don't preach to them or slip in a condemning declaration. I simply thank God that He allowed our paths to cross, and that I hope He would provide us another opportunity to talk about both of our lives and how we can both learn more about Him. I make it brief, simple and sincere. Every person I have done that with has thanked me after the prayer. Some have wiped subtle tears from their eyes. Some have smiled. But everyone has said, "Thank you."

Just do your part
Remember, God may not have you to be the change-agent in their lives. You may be one piece of their life's spiritual puzzle that another will build upon until the Lord determines to bring about life-change in this particular individual. God is the One Who ultimately brings about spiritual maturity in peoples' lives. The apostle Paul reminds us of this very fact in 1 Corinthians 3:5-7 when he talks about other ministers who have engaged a particular group of people:

"After all, who is Apollos? Who is Paul? We are only God's servants through whom you believed the Good News. Each of us did the work the Lord gave us. I planted the seed in your hearts, and Apollos watered it, but it was God who made it grow. It's not important who does the planting, or who does the watering. What's important is that God makes the seed grow."

Begin today
Start having intentional spiritual discussions among those you know well. Ask questions. Listen and learn from others. Study their responses. Don't expect to have all the answers. Then engage someone in your community. Do a lot of listening. Then ask God to guide the discussions into fuller experiences. Pray daily that God will both strengthen your spiritual relationship with Him and also create another disciple in the process.

Study what the Bible says about the Great Commission
I encourage you to further research verses on this topic—Matthew 28:18-20; Mark 16:15-18; Luke 24:44-48; John 20:19-23; Acts 1:3-8.

Write it down... ↘

...& make it
HAPPEN!

RENEWAL

(RI-NOO-UHL)

"This is an integral concept in Christian theology, denoting all those processes of restoration of spiritual strength subsequent to and proceeding from the new birth."
- EVANGELICAL DICTIONARY OF THEOLOGY, 1010

If you say the words "revival" or "renewal" to a group of Christians you will probably get a number of different responses. Some would think of "revival meetings" at their church every summer. Others would picture their weekly church services that emphasize the pouring out of the Holy Spirit. Still some would think of the historical revivals that have appeared throughout the history of the Christian church. Spiritual awakenings such as the First and Second Great Awakening, and the revivals at the turn of the twentieth century would likely come to mind.

For our purposes we will be focusing on the concept of both individual and corporate renewal and revival. Depending on the literature you may be reviewing, or the individual you may address, there are different perspectives when the words "revival" or "renewal" are used. Sometimes the words are used synonymously; other times there is a distinction between the words.

We will be looking at the concept of renewal from the perspective conveyed in passages such as Romans 12:2. As the apostle Paul states, "Don't copy the behavior and customs of this world, but let God transform you into a new person by changing the way you think. Then you will learn to know God's will for you, which is good and pleasing and perfect." The phrase, "but let God transform you into a new person by changing the way you think" is translated "but be transformed by the renewing of your mind" in the NKJV. The Greek word, "anakainōsis," is used in the passage, which means a renewal or renovation.

In the Old Testament the concept is seen in passages like Psalm 103:5 and Isaiah 41:1 (NKJV). Isaiah 40:31 also speaks to renewal in the familiar verse, "But those who trust in the LORD will find new strength. They will soar high on wings like eagles. They will run and not grow weary. They will walk and not faint." The Hebrew word used in the passage is chalaph, which can mean change for the better. It carries with it the idea of renewal.

In connection to the concept of renewal is the idea of regeneration, which is a new birth. Regeneration is a one-time occurrence, when the individual is transformed from spiritual death to spiritual life. Renewal, however, is an

185

ongoing process. Renewal is a day-by-day constant renovation in the life of an individual believer. It is similar in concept to the filling of the Holy Spirit, spoken of in Ephesians 5:18b where the apostle Paul challenges believers to, ". . . be filled with the Holy Spirit." Renewal should be evidenced within the life of the individual as well as within the life of the church. Since the church is made up of individuals, if individuals are being renewed on a daily basis through the work of the Holy Spirit, then the church (corporately) will be renewed as well.

> **" RENEWAL IS A DAY-BY-DAY CONSTANT RENO-VATION IN THE LIFE OF AN INDIVIDUAL BELIEVER. "**

PRACTICAL APPLICATION:

Let the games begin

I enjoy most athletics. I always have. I used to play baseball, softball, basketball and recreational volleyball. I enjoyed the entire experience—going through the prep for the game, the game itself and later reflecting upon the game in order to improve my performance for the next game. I had a healthy balance of competition and enjoyment when I played, so even when I lost a game, I never quite allowed it to ruin my day. I played for the fun of the game and had some great experiences.

One thing you learn quickly in the sports arena is that you will perform your best in the game if you have steadily practiced all week. "Steadily" is the key. Come game day, you will be rusty and off your game if you did not practice steadily throughout the entire week. Without steady practice, the warm ups take longer, and the common drills require a few more run-throughs.

Don't listen to the taunting of the opponent

The Evil One makes every attempt to break your flow of steady practice. Just as an opposing basketball team will call a "time out"—right before you shoot your two free throws (in order to "ice" you before you shoot)—you will never be without the temptation to break the flow of being spiritually disciplined. Probably the first way you'll be tempted is to believe that having one good moment of spiritual activity will carry you through the entire week. Meaning, if you have a great spiritual experience at your church on Sunday, you will be tempted to think it was good enough to last you all week long. But just like a basketball player who will not be satisfied to simply practice one day a week, you will be spiritually rusty if you believe the lie that one profound spiritual experience per week will be adequate to make you a strong believer.

The opposition's game plan
The next temptation will most likely be to believe the lie that you are simply on an "emotional rollercoaster." You will be convinced that your choice to grow closer to Jesus daily is simply a "spontaneous, not-well-thought-through decision," a decision that will never last. Next, most likely you will be tempted to look around at other believers and conclude that they don't exercise themselves spiritually every day—and they look like they're doing just fine— so you don't need to push yourself to maintain a daily routine either. Ultimately, the Evil One's goal is to tempt you in small increments of time—slowly and with perfectly-timed interruptions. But don't listen to the taunting of the opponent; they are all lies. Jesus reminds us of this reality in John 8:44b:

He was a murderer from the beginning. He has always hated the truth, because there is no truth in him. When he lies, it is consistent with his character; for he is a liar and the father of lies.

Do it for the love of the game
I have found that there is virtually a perfect correlation with steady practice habits and one's sincere love of the game. In other words, if you love what you are doing, daily practice is not much of an intrusion in one's schedule. Sure there will be days you will become tired and weary just as Galatians 6:9 promised, "So let's not get tired of doing what is good. At just the right time we will reap a harvest of blessing if we don't give up."

And when it doesn't feel like you are making any progress, let 1 Corinthians 15:58 encourage you. Regardless of how you feel, you are always making progress if you are steadily developing spiritually with God, "So, my dear brothers and sisters, be strong and immovable. Always work enthusiastically for the Lord, for you know that nothing you do for the Lord is ever useless."

You are always in the game so make it count
As you daily commit to stay close to God, you can (and will) grow in your faith! With the Holy Spirit guiding you , each day you can renew your mind and be transformed through meditating on God's Word, prayer, regular discussions of spiritual truths with your friends and family, and the positive influence of other believers in your life. So—make the commitment to be renewed each day!

Study what the Bible says about spiritual renewal
I encourage you to further research verses on this topic—Romans 12:2; Isaiah 40:31; Psalm 103:5; Ephesians 4:20-24.

Write it down... ➘

...& make it
HAPPEN!

INDWELLING/
FILLING OF THE HOLY SPIRIT

(IN-DWEL-ING)

"Let the preacher always confess before he preaches that he relies upon the Holy Spirit. Let him burn his manuscript and depend upon the Holy Spirit. If the Spirit does not come to help him, let him be still and let the people go home and pray that the Spirit will help him next Sunday."
- CHARLES SPURGEON, "The Outpouring of the Holy Spirit"
(Sermon No. 201)

#4

The Holy Spirit's ministry of indwelling and filling consistently evidence themselves throughout both the Old and New Testaments. In the Old Testament the filling of the Holy Spirit is seen when the tabernacle is being constructed (Exodus 31:3, 35:31). The filling is also seen in the words of Isaiah, "The Spirit of the Sovereign LORD is upon me, for the LORD has anointed me to bring good news to the poor. He has sent me to comfort the brokenhearted and to proclaim that captives will be released and prisoners will be freed"(Isaiah 61:1). In the New Testament, the filling of the Holy Spirit is evidenced in passages such as Ephesians 5.

There are many considerations concerning the filling and indwelling of the Holy Spirit. First, a distinction should be drawn between the two concepts. The indwelling of the Holy Spirit is evidenced in passages such as Acts 1:8. This indwelling is something that an individual experiences at the moment of conversion, and it is something that cannot be taken away.

#5

On the other hand, the filling of the Holy Spirit is something that is not permanent. It deals with the aspect of control within the life of the believer. Those who do not follow Jesus are not able to be filled with the Holy Spirit because they are a slave to sin (Romans 6). But, those who follow Jesus are to be living their lives for Him. This is presented in Ephesians 5, where the apostle Paul compares someone being controlled by the influences of alcohol versus being controlled by the Holy Spirit. Just as the entire person can be controlled by alcohol, so the entire person should be controlled by the Spirit.

There are two significant aspects of the Christian life that relate specifically to the working of the Holy Spirit. These two aspects are the topics of spiritual gifts and the fruit of the Spirit. Unfortunately, it seems that we often spend our time focusing on one of these areas and essentially neglect the other. Instead of focusing on the importance of encouraging the develop ment of character (the fruit of the Spirit), we focus most of the attention on spiritual gifts. Please do not understand me to say that we should not talk about spiritual gifts at all. I am simply saying that too often we neglect the idea of character development. Galatians 5:22-23 states, "But the Holy Spirit produces this kind of fruit in our lives: love, joy, peace, patience, kindness, goodness, faithfulness, gentleness, and self-control." I wonder what would happen if followers of Jesus would focus their attention on the filling of the Holy Spirit for the enabling of spiritual service and work and character development.

PRACTICAL APPLICATION:

I love coffee

I love coffee. No, I LOVE coffee! I love the smell of it, the taste of it, and I love sitting next to someone who is drinking it. I love sitting in coffee shops and reading (or writing) books. I love the process of grinding it, brewing it and taste-testing it. I enjoy the relaxed environment coffee promotes. And I love the amount of work I can achieve or leisure I can enjoy with it nearby.

In fact, at this very moment, I am sitting in my favorite coffee shop at the corner of a plaza. There are windows across the entire front and side of the shop, and I have a beautiful view of the Blue Ridge Mountains directly in front of me. I probably would not have to delay my writing deadlines if I would stop pausing to stare at God's magnificent landscape . . . and take another sip of coffee. It is "liquid gold," a French-pressed cup of Organic Shadow Grown Mexican Chiapas coffee. It is smooth as silk and somewhat like drinking velvet. The temperature is just right so that I can sip it without burning myself, but I'm able to watch a strand of steam release itself from the thick porcelain mug. Believe me when I say that it doesn't get any better than that!

[Please hold on while I pause to take another sip.]

Watch the clock

It used to be that I could drink coffee morning, noon and night without it affecting me. I don't know what has changed, but I have recently discovered that the later in the evening I drink it, the more fidgety I get. Whereas before I could drink it all the time and nothing in my evening routine would be interrupted, now I've found that if I drink it late at night, I am not able to sit still—I need to fidget with something or type on the computer in order to work off the effects of the caffeine. It gives me this boost of energy at the most inconvenient time! In a physical way, caffeine controls the tone of the moment and affords me with an increased level of energy. And while it is not advisable to acquire your energy from gallons of coffee a day (though, it does sound attractive!), it does provide that little extra study boost.

Let the Holy Spirit control you

The Bible speaks of the Holy Spirit controlling a person's life by providing a level of spiritual rejuvenation. The Holy Spirit affords a believer the opportunity to ponder spiritual thoughts, study and understand God's Word and conduct intentional spiritual discussions with other believers. At the same time, the Holy Spirit guides the thoughts that should be thought, words that should be spoken and actions that should be performed through intensifying a believer's conviction to spiritual truth. Thus, the believer should make every attempt to be "filled with the Holy Spirit" every morning, noon and night.

> " THE MORE YOU ENJOY THE HOLY SPIRIT CONTROLLING YOUR LIFE, THE MORE IT WILL BECOME A PLACE YOU CAN'T WAIT TO VISIT AGAIN AND AGAIN! "

Basic "how-to's"

While we've share some basic "how-to's" in this book (see the chapters on "Sanctification," "Renewal," "Church Membership," "Repentance"), the way in which the Holy Spirit controls you is when you: (1) confess and repent of all known sin in your life every day; (2) run toward and embrace all of the truths taught in God's Word; (3) hunger and thirst after righteousness (Matthew 5:6) through spiritual discussions, pondering God's truth after reading it, and listening to music that points your thinking to God; (4) don't allow anything else to control your thinking. Don't open your mind, heart or emotions to anything that will ultimately boost your energy to pursue sin. Run from those influences—it isn't worth it. The more you enjoy the Holy Spirit controlling your life, the more it will become a place you can't wait to visit again and again!

Study what the Bible says about the indwelling and filling of the Holy Spirit

Here are some more verses to read on this topic—Galatians 5:16-26; Acts 1:8; 1 Corinthians 3:16, 6:19, 12:1-11; Romans 12:3-8; John 14:15-18.

Write it down... ⟶

...& make it
HAPPEN!

LIFE ON MISSION

(MISH-UHN)

"Either way, Christ's love controls us. Since we believe that
Christ died for all, we also believe that we have all died to our
old life. He died for everyone so that those who receive his new
life will no longer live for themselves. Instead, they will live for
Christ, who died and was raised for them."
- 2 CORINTHIANS 5:14-15

In 2002 Pastor Rick Warren released a book entitled, The Purpose-Driven
Life. The book quickly became a national best seller. The book is written as
a devotional and walks its readers through forty days of finding purpose
in their lives. The book talks (as the title would suggest) about living one's
life with purpose. It speaks of being intentional about what you and I are
doing with the time God has given us here on this earth. Regardless of
your personal position on Rev. Rick Warren, I think he has identified a goal
that every believer should be striving for; namely, live your life according to
God's intentional mission for your life.

The apostle Paul is an example of a person who lived his life on mission.
Consider the way in which he described his life in 2 Corinthians 11:1-12:13. In
this passage he talks about the trials and tribulations that he has suffered
for the sake of the gospel of Jesus. He talks about how he has struggled
on behalf of other followers of Jesus. It is as though when they suffered, he
suffered with them. Many times throughout Paul's letters he makes a statement that shows the focus of his ministry, "And you should imitate me, just
as I imitate Christ" (1 Corinthians 11:1). A similar idea is expressed elsewhere
in the writings of Paul (see 1 Corinthians 4:16; Ephesians 5:1; Philippians 3:17,
4:9). Paul realizes that his life is a testimony of the grace of Jesus, but he is
also an example for others to follow. Paul was confident in Jesus' working
through his life to bring glory to God.

Jesus is also an example of living one's life on mission. In the book of John
we see this especially emphasized. There are many times in the book
when Jesus makes the statement, "My time has not yet come" (see John
2:4, 7:30, 8:20, 12:23, 12:27, 13:1). The "time" Jesus was talking about was
the time when He would accomplish the task that He came to earth to do,
which was His death and resurrection. This does not mean that Jesus did
not accomplish other things throughout His time on earth, but it is to say
that He was focused on the main purpose—to die for the sins of the world
and then be resurrected. In John 17:1, we see that Jesus' time had come.
The verse reads, "After saying all these things, Jesus looked up to heaven

and said, 'Father, the hour has come. Glorify your Son so he can give glory back to you.'" Jesus knew His hour how come, and He was prepared for that time.

My fear is that you and I wander through life without a purpose. I'm concerned that many of us go through this life without really thinking about what it is we are trying to accomplish—nor do we let God accomplish His purpose through us. I think all too often we just go through the motions of life. We go from one thing to the next without really being on mission. My hope and my prayer is that you will take a serious look at the focus of your life and start to intentionally live a life of purpose—a life that is on mission for Jesus and for God's glory.

PRACTICAL APPLICATION:

Plan to focus . . . then focus on your plan

In the middle of a discussion about the cost of being a disciple of Jesus Christ, Jesus shared an analogy of how important it is to consider the level to which you are involved in something before you engage in the initiative. And one of the things Jesus accomplished when sharing the following analogies in Luke 14:28-32 was to show His disciples that it is wise to have a plan before you attempt to execute:

> "BUT DON'T BEGIN UNTIL YOU COUNT THE COST. For who would begin construction of a building without first calculating the cost to see if there is enough money to finish it? Otherwise, you might complete only the foundation before running out of money, and then everyone would laugh at you. They would say, 'There's the person who started that building and couldn't afford to finish it!' Or what king would go to war against another king without first sitting down with his counselors to discuss whether his army of 10,000 could defeat the 20,000 soldiers marching against him?"

It is difficult to miss the common-sense approach that Jesus was conveying to His listeners—if you don't plan well before you execute, you will lose money, be defeated and be embarrassed.

Many others have recognized this reality in day-to-day life. This commonly quoted axiom has been adopted by virtually every leader in every sector of life:

> "If you aim at nothing, you are certain to hit it!"

So many people have quoted a version of the above statement it is difficult to identify the original source, but that's the point—most everyone identifies with the reality of this saying. If you don't have a plan, you will "successfully" waffle around in an ill-focused manner and accomplish nothing of eternal purpose or personal edification.

The real power is behind the plan

While it is helpful to default naturally to a planning mentality, organization alone does not equal spirituality. Just because you are the most analytical person in the room, or you can't sit in a room for two seconds without cleaning it, or you have to organize everything on the nightstand—none of that makes you a spiritual person. Remember, your spiritual success does not rest in the power of your planning skills, but it is in direct proportion to the time you intentionally engage in God's Word, in spiritual discussions, and in prayer. In addition, your spiritual progress is not determined by the amount of hours logged in as "devotional" time as much as in the quality of those experiences with God and with others.

> **'SPIRITUALITY' WILL NEVER SIMPLY 'HAPPEN' TO YOU.**

Make it count

There are many practical spiritual activities to make sure quality time gets accomplished in your life (see the chapters on "Sanctification," "Renewal," "Church Membership," "Repentance," "Indwelling/Filling of the Holy Spirit"). But what will permit those activities to really impact your life is to ask the Holy Spirit to grant you wisdom to shift/move/cancel/add various agenda items in your weekly schedule and to intentionally insert spiritual activities/thoughts/words/actions into your day. Then stick to that commitment.

Allow this truth to motivate you to stick to your plan—"Spirituality" will never simply "happen" to you. You must intentionally engage the Holy Spirit in spiritual activity in order to see spiritual results.

Study what the Bible says about living your life according to God's mission

Here are some more verses to read on this topic—2 Corinthians 11:22-33; Psalm 101; 1 Corinthians 6:20, 7:23, 10:31-33, 11:1; Colossians 2:23-24.

Write it down... ↘

...& make it
HAPPEN!

END TIMES

ASCENSION

(UH-SEN-SHUHN)

"After saying this, he was taken up into a cloud while they were
watching, and they could no longer see him."
- ACTS 1:9

There if often a focus on the resurrection of Jesus Christ, and rightfully so,
as it is a defining point in human history. Paul says in 1 Corinthians 15:14 that
"if Christ has not been raised, then all our preaching is useless, and your
faith is useless." But, there is also great significance to the ascension of
Jesus Christ. We learn four important things from the ascension of Christ:

First, we learn that the work Jesus came to earth to complete was in fact completed

Throughout the book of John there is a statement repeated by Jesus,
"My time has not yet come" (see John 2:4, 7:30, 8:20, 12:23, 12:27, 13:1).
We looked at this phrase in the previous chapter regarding Jesus living
on mission, but this particular phrase also refers to the timing of His final
ascension. In John 17:1, right before His arrest, trials and crucifixion, Jesus
prays to the Father and says, "Father, the hour has come"—His mission is
complete and it is time for Jesus to return to heaven (the ascension). Jesus
knew that He came to earth to die on the cross for the sins of the world
and that He would be raised again for victory over death. Since this work
has been completed, Jesus now arrives back in heaven where He is seated
at the right hand of God the Father (Psalm 110:1).

Second, we learn that Jesus is preparing an eternal home for those who believe in Him

Jesus said in John 14:1-4 that He would be going to heaven to prepare a
place for His followers, and He would come again so that His followers
may be with Him in heaven. This preparation carries with it many analogies to the preparation an engaged man in the first century would take in
preparing for his wife. He would take time to prepare their home before the
wedding ceremony. In a similar way, the Bridegroom (Jesus) is preparing a
dwelling place for His bride (the church). The analogy of the church being
the bride of Christ is evident within Scripture, especially in passages like
Ephesians 5:23-32 and 2 Corinthians 11:2-4.

Third, the ascension of Christ prepares the way for the current ministry of the Holy Spirit

The Holy Spirit is evident in the Old Testament (see Isaiah 61:1), but the ministry of the Holy Spirit is seen more prevalently in the New Testament after

the ascension of Jesus. I have often thought that it is at this point in Scripture that some of us may have a hard time trusting in the words of Jesus. In John 16:7 Jesus says, ". . . it is best for you that I go away, because if I don't, the Advocate won't come. If I do go away, then I will send him to you." Are we really committed to trusting Jesus when He says that it is better for Him to go away, so that the Holy Spirit will come?

Finally, the ascension of Jesus is an example of the future for those who believe in Jesus
Just as Jesus died, was buried, rose again and ascended into heaven to be with the Father, so also will those who believe in Jesus ascend to heaven to be with the Father for all eternity. The Bible indicates that Jesus' followers were baptized into His death and were raised to walk in newness of life (Romans 6:3-4). And in 1 Corinthians 15:50-58 we read about the future time when followers of Jesus will be with Him in heaven.

Truly the ascension of Jesus is a significant point in the course of Jesus' ministry. It is recognition of Jesus' accomplishment of the work He came to do on earth, and it sets the stage for His current primary ministry as the advocate on behalf of His followers.

PRACTICAL APPLICATION:

Parting is such sweet sorrow
If you ever want a cheap source of light-hearted entertainment—and a quick laugh—walk down the hallway of your church's nursery and observe the parents that are dropping off their children for an hour or two. You can tell the parents that have more than one child and regularly attend church. They make the transition smoothly—hand off the child, sign them in, gather all of the required security items, give their child a warm hug, blow their child a kiss and away they go to the church service. Then there are the first-time parents and the visitors—arrive at the door, hug their child, sign in the child, hug their child again, look past the nursery worker (as she attempts to describe the security policies) to evaluate the cleanliness of nursery facility, embrace the child even tighter and reluctantly hand the child over the half-door that divides the nursery from the hallway. The child runs along with great excitement to play with the other children as long faces appear on the parents' faces. But don't leave the scene yet, as these same parents will be there two minutes from now squashing their noses against the glass attempting to find the best angle to view their child at play through any gap they can find in the venetian blinds. You may even see a tear on the face(s) of the parent(s) as one usually gains more strength to encourage the other to finally leave the vicinity.

The reunion is sweet
After the service is over (or possibly before the service concludes) these

new parents and visitors hustle to greet their child with open arms. The parents cannot sign the paperwork and exchange the security items quick enough, anxious to get his/her hands on the child. The child is greeted with a huge, warm hug as the other parent comes around and sandwiches the child with another hug from the other side. And even though this moment makes "veteran" parents smile and reminisce of former days, the moment is sweet to observe. In the context of this chapter, this scene serves as a powerful reminder of a sweet reunion that the ascension of Jesus Christ promises us.

I'll be back

Forty days after Jesus died and physically and bodily rose again from the dead, He ascended (literally, "transported Himself") back to heaven. He had some encouraging parting words for His disciples and all believers. Jesus promised that the Holy Spirit would come and be the ever-presence of God in their lives—just as Jesus Christ was the presence of God Himself to them for these past thirty-three years upon the earth. (In fact, we see a vivid picture of the "Trinity" or "Tri-unity" of the Godhead in Jesus' comments to His disciples upon His ascension—just as we saw in Jesus' baptism (Matthew 3:16-17)). But Jesus also made a promise of a certain return to gather His children to Himself (see the chapter on "Return of Jesus Christ").

And for us, many years have passed and every believer has longed for the return of the Lord. Of course, God has His own timetable and has decided not to return yet. Because of this perceived "delay" in Jesus' return, many unbelievers have done just what the apostle Peter assured us would happen:

> "MOST IMPORTANTLY, I WANT TO REMIND YOU that in the last days scoffers will come, mocking the truth and following their own desires. They will say, "What happened to the promise that Jesus is coming again? From before the times of our ancestors, everything has remained the same since the world was first created" (2 Peter 3:3-4).

But one thing is certain—and every believer can take 100 percent confidence in this promise—that just as certain as Jesus left this world to return to heaven, Jesus will, with equal certainty, return to gather us to Himself (see the chapter on "Return of Jesus Christ"). And even though the Lord could be likened to a "veteran" parent who has many, many children upon this earth, the Lord still retains that new-parent excitement to be reunited again with us! Psalm 139:17-18 assures every believer of this reality:

> "HOW PRECIOUS ARE YOUR THOUGHTS ABOUT ME, O GOD. They cannot be numbered! I can't even count them; they outnumber the grains of sand! And when I wake up, you are still with me!"

" TAKE A MOMENT TO TALK TO GOD ABOUT
YOUR FEELINGS REGARDING HIS RETURN. ASK
THE LORD TO INCREASE YOUR DESIRE FOR HIM
TO RETURN SOON. **"**

Share in the excitement
Take a moment to think about all that Jesus did upon this earth leading up
to His ascension. Thank Him in your prayers for the sacrifice of His own life
on the cross and for His amazing resurrection (see the chapter on "Salvation"). Then tell Jesus how much you miss Him and long to see Him. Take
a moment to talk to God about your feelings regarding His return. Ask the
Lord to increase your desire for Him to return soon. If you do this, you'll
find that the more you read the Bible, have intentional discussions with fellow believers about God's truth and share the realities of Jesus Christ with
others, you will have true longing for His return. And consider ending your
prayers to God with a sincere request to come soon—similar to the words
that the apostle John prayed to God in the very last book of the Bible:

> HE WHO IS THE FAITHFUL WITNESS TO ALL THESE THINGS says, "Yes, I am com-
> ing soon!" "Amen! Come, Lord Jesus" (Revelation 22:20).

Study what the Bible says about the ascension of Jesus Christ
Here are some more verses to read on this topic—John 20:17; Mark 16:19-
20; Luke 24:49-53; Acts 1:9.

Write it down... ↘

...& make it
HAPPEN!

CHRIST AS ADVOCATE

(AD-VUH-KIT)

"Jesus' current ministry is a great source of comfort, authority, and encouragement for the believers because it ensures that his ministry as Prophet, Priest, and King continues and will one day be acknowledged by all creation."
- ESV STUDY BIBLE, 2526

After accomplishing the work on earth that Jesus came to do (namely His death, burial and resurrection), He sat down at the right hand of God the Father (Matthew 26:64). But, this does not mean that Jesus is not doing anything in His current ministry in heaven. The primary ministry of Jesus is now a ministry of intercession for those who follow Him.

Intercession is a concept that is typically associated with the ministry of a priest. In the Old Testament, the priest would make intercession for the people of Israel (see Leviticus 1-6). Today, believers in Jesus have Him as their Great High Priest who intercedes for them (see Hebrews 4:14-5:11). Picture Satan, the great deceiver, bringing charges of sin against the people of God, and Jesus is seated next to the Father saying, "I have paid the price for that sin." Jesus is the One who stands in our place; He is the One who comes to our defense when charges are brought against us.

The term that is used in 1 John 2:1 is advocate. John says, "My dear children, I am writing this to you so that you will not sin. But if anyone does sin, we have an advocate who pleads our case before the Father. He is Jesus Christ, the one who is truly righteous." The Greek word for advocate is paraklētos, which used in this context means, "to plead another's cause." Elsewhere in Scripture, the same word is used of the ministry and work of the Holy Spirit. In John 16:7, Jesus says that He will send the paraklētos after Jesus ascends into heaven.

Romans 8:34 reads, "Who then will condemn us? No one—for Christ Jesus died for us and was raised to life for us, and he is sitting in the place of honor at God's right hand, pleading for us." It is because of this ministry of Jesus that His followers do not need to fear the condemnation of the Devil. You and I can confidently approach God the Father as His child and as a co-heir with Christ (see Romans 8:16-17).

Romans chapter 8 concludes with the following words from the apostle Paul, "And I am convinced that nothing can ever separate us from God's love. Neither death nor life, neither angels nor demons, neither our fears for today nor our worries about tomorrow—not even the powers of hell can separate us from God's love. No power in the sky above or in the earth below—indeed, nothing in all creation will ever be able to separate us from the love of God that is revealed in Christ Jesus our Lord." Paul says these words, not because of the things that we have done in our own ability, but because of what Jesus has done on our behalf (His death, burial and resurrection), as well as His current ministry of intercession. It is not because of you and I that we are saved and stand uncondemned. No, it is because of the love and work of Jesus.

PRACTICAL APPLICATION:

Child's play
Children are notorious for attempting to persuade their parents to provide equal (or better) blessings to them when their sibling receives a blessing. If you give one child a reward for doing a good job on a math test, the other one will inevitably ask for the same reward by saying, "It's unfair that he gets that and I don't . . . " And the more the parent explains the reason for why the brother or sister received the reward, the more the other child will say, "But it's not fair . . . they shouldn't get that if I can't . . . it's not fair." Then out of jealousy or rivalry or competition, the appeal turns into accusations. "But Mom, he doesn't deserve to get that because you remember last week when he [fill in the blank], and you got so mad at him . . . he shouldn't still get that reward!"

And almost every parent at that moment thinks back to how the two children were so loving to each other just the other day, but now they are throwing each other under the bus and accusing each other of being "unworthy" to receive a blessing from the parent. After concluding that there is no discernible explanation for this swing of emotions, we as parents simply make one more attempt to explain why we have decided to continue to lavish their other sibling with love and rewards—regardless of the amount of mistakes that the other child has resurrected and begged the parent to rehearse in his/her memory.

Satan's futile attempts
Just like immature children, Satan makes the same attempt to accuse us before our Lord and Savior, Jesus Christ, making the case that we are unworthy of remaining children of God. Fortunately, Satan will never be able to persuade God that we are unworthy to be called His children.

Satan is powerful, but He is not God! He may be stronger than most all created beings, but he must stand mute when the Almighty God of the universe speaks on our behalf. At his core, Satan is an accuser (in fact, his name means "the one who accuses"). And he will stop at nothing to attempt to make a case to God that any and all believers are not worthy to

**" SATAN WILL NEVER BE ABLE TO PERSUADE
GOD THAT WE ARE UNWORTHY TO BE CALLED
HIS CHILDREN. "**

be the recipients of God's saving grace (see the chapter on "Salvation"). Satan approached God when he wanted to touch Job's life (Job 1-2). He also had the gall to approach Jesus and accuse Him of doing things the wrong way early in Jesus' earthly ministry (Matthew 4). Satan approached Jesus in an attempt to "sift" (i.e., challenge to the point of overthrowing) Peter and the disciples' faith the night before Jesus' crucifixion (Luke 22:31). And he even dares to approach your Savior, the Lord Jesus Christ, to accuse you "day and night" of being unworthy of your salvation (Revelation 12:10). Fortunately, neither Satan nor anyone else will ever be able to present a persuasive case to God the Father to release His grip upon a believer's soul. Why? Because once Jesus Christ has settled the issue through His atoning work on the cross (see the chapter on "Salvation"), Jesus will forever win any arguments regarding a believer's justification (see the chapter on "Justification").

An indelible promise

ROMANS 8:33-39 IS ONE OF THE MOST MARVELOUS PORTIONS OF THE BIBLE that provides immeasurable comfort and protection for all believers. In fact, many have memorized the following passage: Who dares accuse us whom God has chosen for his own? No one—for God himself has given us right standing with himself. Who then will condemn us? No one—for Christ Jesus died for us and was raised to life for us, and he is sitting in the place of honor at God's right hand, pleading for us. Can anything ever separate us from Christ's love? Does it mean he no longer loves us if we have trouble or calamity, or are persecuted, or hungry, or destitute, or in danger, or threatened with death? (As the Scriptures say, "For your sake we are killed every day; we are being slaughtered like sheep.") No, despite all these things, overwhelming victory is ours through Christ, who loved us. And I am convinced that nothing can ever separate us from God's love. Neither death nor life, neither angels nor demons, neither our fears for today nor our worries about tomorrow—not even the powers of hell can separate us from God's love. No power in the sky above or in the earth below—indeed, nothing in all creation will ever be able to separate us from the love of God that is revealed in Christ Jesus our Lord."

Experiencing tangible peace

Knowing Jesus is the Advocate for all believers should affect our lives in a very tangible way. This reality should serve as your fixed point of reference. It ought to provide deep peace in your heart when you feel that you have dishonored God with your decisions as a believer. Knowing that God will keep you accountable and may bring people into your life to provide spiritual redirection for your own good (see the chapter on "Church"), He does this because you are His child . . . and He loves you. Romans 8:33-39 is a great passage to memorize, so you can rehearse this God-inspired promise when you begin to feel "unworthy" as God's child. Live up to your name—a child of God. Stop listening to the lies of the Devil that you are unworthy to be called a child of God (1 John 3:1) and begin to listen to the Holy Spirit Who will always draw you back to the promise of this reality!

Study what the Bible says about Christ as the believer's Advocate
I encourage you to further research verses on this topic—1 John 2:1; Hebrews 4:14-5:11; Revelation 12:10; Matthew 26:64; Acts 7:55-56.

Write it down... ⟶

...& make it
HAPPEN!

RETURN OF JESUS CHRIST

(AD-VUH-KIT)

"'Men of Galilee,' they said, 'why are you standing here staring into heaven? Jesus has been taken from you into heaven, but someday he will return from heaven in the same way you saw him go!'"
- ACTS 1:11

There is much debate about when, and how, Jesus will return to earth, but there is a consistent agreement throughout church history that Jesus is returning. This confidence is due to the overwhelming evidence that supports this claim, especially in the New Testament writings. Over twenty of the twenty-seven books in the New Testament mention the second coming of Jesus. It is one of the consistent and prevalent themes in the teachings of Jesus, the apostles, and the early church fathers. Matthew 24 and 25 recorded Jesus' statements about the kingdom of God, and in John 14:3 Jesus comforts His disciples by letting them know that, "When everything is ready, I will come and get you, so that you will always be with me where I am."

One of the Greek terms used in regard to the second coming is found in 1 Thessalonians 4:15. The word is parousia, which means, "presence, coming or arrival." Other words used to convey the return of Jesus are apokalypsis, meaning "revelation" and also epiphaneia, which means "appearance" or "manifestation." Theologically, the return of Jesus is significant to our understanding of future events. Among the important considerations are the following aspects:

First, the second coming of Jesus will be a bodily and personal coming of the Lord. Acts 1:11 makes the statement, ". . . someday he will return from heaven in the same way you saw him go." This seems to indicate that it will be a physical return to earth. In addition, the second coming of Jesus is spoken of by Paul within the context of the resurrection from the dead, which stresses the bodily nature of the resurrection (1 Corinthians 15).

Second, the significance of the second coming of Jesus can be seen in both the establishment of His kingdom and in His judgment of all of humanity. Scripture indicates a future literal reign of Jesus on the earth, as well as a future literal judgment. It was prophesied in the Old Testament that the heir of David would reign forever on the throne of David, and Jesus is the fulfillment of that prophesy (see 2 Samuel 7:4-17). Jesus is the "shoot of Jesse" spoken of in Isaiah 11, where it is foretold that Jesus will rule the world.

Finally, as significant as the establishment of His kingdom on earth will be in the end times, it is also amazing to consider the fact that Jesus has not left us alone on our earthly journey—He has not forgotten about you and me. But rather, Jesus desires that you and I spend eternity with Him. He is coming back again, so that we may be where He is—for all eternity.

> **❝ SCRIPTURE INDICATES A FUTURE LITERAL REIGN OF JESUS ON THE EARTH, AS WELL AS A FUTURE LITERAL JUDGMENT. ❞**

In His first coming, Jesus came as a humble baby, born of the Virgin Mary on an eventless night in Bethlehem. At His second coming, Jesus will return as a conquering King. He will lead His people to victory and establish His Kingdom.

PRACTICAL APPLICATION:

Clipping coupons

During my childhood years, our family did not have a lot of money. And in those days the only way to receive a discounted price at the grocery store was to cut out coupons from the newspaper or magazines that were delivered to the house daily. I recall my mother "clipping coupons" religiously everyday—especially on the weekends—in order to find all the discounts possible on a certain product from every available newspaper or magazine. On many occasions, I recall her showing me the stack of coupons and being so excited that she found multiple coupons for the same product. To her, it was thrilling to find a coupon that exceeded fifty cents—that was indeed a big deal!

Grocery stores soon began to adopt yet another marketing effort by which to lure customers like my mother into their particular store—"Double Coupon Days!" This was publicized when a store decided to offer any customer double the discount on any coupon (usually up to fifty cents or one dollar). You can imagine the excitement level of my mother when she would drive by and see a store advertising this limited-time offer. If driving, she would often brake immediately, in her excitement, and turn into the parking lot in order to redeem her coupons for double the value—almost causing an eighteen-car-pile-up behind her! To my mom, it was a deal that could not be passed up. And even if her preferred grocery shopping day was not for another three days, this deal-of-a-lifetime could not be ignored. She would redeem every coupon right then and there.

The day of redemption

Knowing every human analogy falls apart at some moment, I liken the promise of the return of Christ to someone who has been given a coupon that is redeemable on a "special day." Jesus Christ has saved our souls and has promised that there will be a day that He Himself will return for us—to collect the ones whom He saved. The Bible calls this day, the "day of redemption." Ephesians 4:30b mentions this day, "Remember, he has identified you as his own, guaranteeing that you will be saved on the day of redemption." There was a day that Jesus Christ offered redemption to you (cf. the coupon in the paper).

There was a day that Jesus Christ's redemption was yours (cf. the day you clipped it out of the newspaper). And ultimately there will be a day when you will experience the promise of heaven that His redemption provides (see 1 Thessalonians 4:11-18).Jesus will physically and literally return to gather you from the earth and take you to heaven. "Then we will be with the Lord forever" (v. 17).

Allow tomorrow to give you hope today

Confidence of tomorrow should provide you with spiritual stability today. The more you study the return of Christ, the more you should be filled with hope that God is at work in your life today. One of the favorite Bible verses of the late Founding Chancellor/President of Liberty University, Dr. Jerry Falwell, Sr. was Philippians 1:6. There were many reasons why he valued this verse, not the least of which was the fact that this verse gives hope that God will never stop working in a believer's life while he/she is upon the earth. It also provides a promise that there will be a day when every believer will be in the literal, physical presence of Jesus! The verse reads:

And I am certain that God, who began the good work within you, will continue his work until it is finally finished on the day when Christ Jesus returns.

If God Himself is indeed able to return for you and take you to heaven, then He loves you enough and is powerful enough to protect, provide, develop and mature you in your spiritual walk today.

Allow the return of Christ to comfort you

The return of Christ should not be a cause for anxiety in the heart of a believer. The return of Jesus Christ was referenced by the apostle Paul on many occasions to provide emotional comfort for believers. In fact, every chapter in the book of 1 Thessalonians ends with a reference or inference to the return of Jesus Christ. Most notably is 1 Thessalonians 4:13-18 that describes the return of Jesus Christ in vivid detail. Paul concludes with the clear instruction for believers to teach others about the return of Christ. His guaranteed return should both motivate believers to live their lives to please Christ as well as bring comfort to us while we wait—"So encourage each other with these words" (v.18).

Study what the Bible says about the return of Jesus Christ
I encourage you to further research verses on this topic—Matthew 24-25; 1 Thessalonians 4:15; Acts 1:11; Titus 2:13.

Write it down... ↘

...& make it
HAPPEN!

THIRTY NINE

HEAVEN

(HEV-UHN)

"Heaven is the place where God most fully makes known his presence to bless."
- WAYNE GRUDEM, Bible Doctrine, 485

Trying to describe heaven in a few short pages is no small challenge. Fortunately, it is not left up to you or me to imagine what heaven will be like. God provides us with a description of heaven, and although it's not exhaustive, this description gives us a picture of the eternal resting place of those who believe in Jesus.

How do we define heaven? Is it the dwelling place of God? Is it freedom from sin? The actual Greek word that is used in the New Testament is, ouranos. It can be used to mean the stellar heavens, the expanse, or as is the case in Revelation 21:1-2, it means the place where God and the heavenly beings dwell. We see a picture of this dwelling place of God throughout the Old and New Testaments. Isaiah describes the vision he experienced of the throne room of God when he received his call to be a prophet. Isaiah 6 records the vision and provides us with a picture of the heavenly angels (seraphim) who encircle the throne of God, as well as a picture of God seated on His throne. When Stephen was being martyred in the New Testament, he saw the throne room of God with Jesus standing at the right hand of God the Father (Acts 7).

Although there are many significance aspects of heaven that could be covered, three have been specifically selected to focus our attention. The first is the understanding that heaven is a real place. Heaven is a place where followers of Jesus will bodily spend all of eternity. The apostle Paul makes the bodily nature of this eternal home very clear in 1 Corinthians 15:53 when he says, "For our dying bodies must be transformed into bodies that will never die; our mortal bodies must be transformed into immortal bodies." This discussion relates to the person of Jesus and His experiences after the resurrection. It is clear from Scripture that Jesus was bodily raised from the dead, and Scripture indicates that He ascended into heaven, further verifying the bodily nature of the eternal state.

A second important consideration about heaven is that it is eternal. Jesus often spoke of "eternal life." In Matthew 25:46, He uses the Greek term, aiōnios, which means without ending or everlasting, to describe the future of both the righteous and the unrighteous. In this verse Jesus said, "And they will go away into eternal punishment, but the righteous will go into eternal life."

In addition to understanding that heaven is a real place and heaven is for eternity, the third important aspect to remember is that heaven signifies being in the presence of Jesus. In the notes on heaven in the ESV Study Bible the statement is included, "Fellowship with Jesus, it has been said, is what makes heaven to be heaven, and that is something that Christian people will be proving true for all eternity" (2534). Even though there are great rewards in heaven, the greatest reward is being in the presence of Jesus.

> **EVEN THOUGH THERE ARE GREAT REWARDS IN HEAVEN, THE GREATEST REWARD IS BEING IN THE PRESENCE OF JESUS.**

PRACTICAL APPLICATION:

A powerful memory
A few years ago, I gathered with my family to celebrate the life of my precious grandmother. She was a special woman who had a large family and worked tirelessly to help my grandpa provide throughout the years. She was also a devoted Christian and taught all of us by her personal example how to trust God in all things—no matter what. Her handwritten letters to each individual family member were instant keepsakes as they oozed with Bible references and practical applications and encouragements. Near the end of her life, she often wrote that she desired to remain with us and enjoy our fellowship one more year. But in the next sentence you could sense her excitement as she dreamed about going "home" to be with her Lord and Savior. She would then return to the topic at hand and address certain things that related to us as her grandchildren. Soon, however, once again we would catch her mind turning her focus to the joy that heaven would one day provide for her. These mixed emotions would happen in virtually every letter she sent us.

A sign of spiritual stability
My grandmother's shifting of emotions—from wanting to stay here on earth with her loved ones to longing to be in heaven with her Savior—was not an exhibition of an unstable person. In fact, it was just the opposite. It was a very practical example of how you can both deeply love the people that God has given you during your earthly life and also love God with all your heart, longing to be with your Savior in heaven.

In all reality, believers in Jesus Christ who have grasped the fact that all good things in this life come directly from God Himself (James 1:17) will long to fellowship with the precious family of God to which they belong (see the chapter on "Ecclesia" and "Church Membership"). In addition, any believer who has truly grasped the depth of the sacrifice of the Lord Jesus Christ in order to provide salvation for his/her sins (see the chapter on "Christology") will long to be in heaven with the Lord.

I want to go home

My grandmother was not alone in her two-fold desire to "stay" and "go." The apostle Paul felt these same emotions. And just like our family appreciated reading my grandmother's thoughts about us along with her thoughts about heaven, the apostle exhibited the same emotions before his close friends in Philippi, and they grew from reading his letter:

> "FOR TO ME, LIVING MEANS LIVING FOR CHRIST, and dying is even better. But if I live, I can do more fruitful work for Christ. So I really don't know which is better. I'm torn between two desires: I long to go and be with Christ, which would be far better for me. But for your sakes, it is better that I continue to live" (Philippians 1:21-24).

Living in a constant conundrum

A mature believer in Jesus Christ will always experience this life-long conundrum. Paul returns to this theme once again later on in his letter to his friends in Philippi:

> "BUT WE ARE CITIZENS OF HEAVEN, where the Lord Jesus Christ lives. And we are eagerly waiting for him to return as our Savior. He will take our weak mortal bodies and change them into glorious bodies like his own, using the same power with which he will bring everything under his control" (Philippians 3:20-21).

Tomorrow affects us today

Here are some simple, practical biblical encouragements regarding how the reality of heaven should affect you today:

1. Don't fear heaven

It may sound silly, but some people do fear this supernatural transition from physically dwelling upon the earth to immediately joining the Lord Jesus Christ in heaven. This ought not to be so. If you are a believer in Jesus Christ (this is an important "if"), then heaven is a glorious place full of comfort, satisfaction and true peace (see the chapter on "Salvation").

2. Don't forget heaven

While you are enjoying the blessings of God on this earth, don't allow your focus to be consumed with the "now" and the stuff of today. It is quite alright to want to accomplish certain goals in this world, but it will never ever deflate any excitement about the things of today if you spend more time anticipating being with God someday.

3. Don't forget how you inherited heaven

The joy of today and the promise of tomorrow should cause you to thank God daily for all He has done to make these joys possible. Take time today—in your car, on a walk, during your study time, etc.—to offer a prayer to God and thank Him for all He has done for you.

Study what the Bible says about heaven

Here are some more verses to read on this topic—Isaiah 65:17; 2 Peter 3:13; Revelation 21; Ephesians 5:5.

Write it down... →

...& make it HAPPEN!

FORTY

HELL

> "If there is one basic characteristic of hell, it is, in contrast
> to heaven, the absence of God or banishment from his pres-
> ence. It is an experience of intense anguish, whether it involves
> physical suffering or mental distress or both."
> - MILLARD ERICKSON, Christian Theology (1242)

Many times in Jesus' ministry on earth He talked about the kingdom of
God, but He also talked about those who did not believe in Him. Throughout His teachings Jesus talked about the eternal resting place of those who
would not follow Him. Although it is sometimes a difficult topic to discuss,
it is very important that we process through the destiny of those who
continue not to believe in Jesus as their Savior. Matthew 25 provides a vivid
picture of the eternal home of those who refuse to place their faith in Jesus.
Hell is described in Scripture as a place of "outer darkness" (v. 30), a place
of "eternal fire" (v. 41), and a place of "eternal punishment" (v. 46) There are
many words used in the Bible to describe the place, including sheol (Psalm
18:5), hades (Luke 16), tartaros (2 Peter 2:4), and gehenna (Luke 12:5).

The most severe of these words is gehanna, which is the eternal resting
place of souls. The word was first used of a valley near the city of Jerusalem known as the Valley of Hinnom, which was used as a place where the
waste and dead animals from the city were taken to be burned. Throughout the New Testament, gehenna is used of the eternal dwelling place of
those who do not place their faith in Jesus. Whereas hades and sheol are
used to describe a place for individuals before the final judgment, gehenna
is used to describe the "lake of fire" described in Revelation 20.

Two very important aspects of hell should be considered in our study:

Hell is a place of eternal separation from God
Just as heaven is eternal fellowship with God, hell is a place of eternal separation from God. As Wayne Grudem states in his book, Bible Doctrine, "We
may define hell as follows: Hell is a place of eternal conscious punishment
for the wicked" (459). Although some may want to teach that everyone
will eventually be saved (known as universalism), or that hell is not eternal
(known as annihilationism), Scripture does not allow for either of those
options. As has previously been mentioned, Matthew 25 specifically states
that hell is eternal.

Hell is a place of no hope
There are no second chances for those who are in hell. Luke 16:9-31 records

a story that Jesus told concerning a rich man and a beggar named Lazarus. In the story, both men die and go to eternity. The rich man is said to be in great torment, but no relief is given to him. This story describes the level of eternal torment as well as his desire for no one else from his family to come to this horrible place. The description is self-explanatory as you observe that in hell he has retained his memory, senses (i.e., see, touch, taste, thirst, etc.), is in torment and is convinced of the truth of his need for salvation that was presented to him when he was alive upon the earth. The devastating fact of hell is that it is forever, and there is no hope of a change. You and I can face many challenges in our lifetime, but nothing we go through here on earth compares to the torments of hell, because there is no relief from an eternity in hell.

> **" THE DEVASTATING FACT OF HELL IS THAT IT IS FOREVER, AND THERE IS NO HOPE OF A CHANGE. "**

PRACTICAL APPLICATION:

A frequently asked question

One does not have to be a teacher for long to experience the following scenario. As an educator, I occasionally get the following response from students who have received failing grades. After the semesters ends, there always seems to be at least one student who emails me something like, "I just looked up my grades and saw that I received a failing grade for your class. Why did you fail me?"

Of course, I review with the student his/her grades along with the instructions that were either ignored or not specifically followed. I also review the feedback that I had provided the student on any assignments that were turned in. Then I tally the amount of effort that the student made to pursue outside tutoring and study groups (if applicable). And lastly, I identify the number of extensions that were provided for the student over the course of the class. But even then, after we reviewed all of the rubrics, grades and correspondences between the student and me, the same question often comes up again, "Why did you decide to fail me?" Which really means, "Why did you do this to me?"

Hell is a choice

The unfortunate reality is that I did not fail the student—the student failed himself/herself. Each student knows the requirements, occasionally experiences mercy and patience with regard to deadlines, is offered clarity as to the requirements that are incumbent upon the student to adhere to, and is given great levels of encouragement to abide by the requirements of the class. But in the end, it is the student who chooses not to abide by the parameters set by the professor in the class. (Quite honestly, I hate using this analogy because I don't like to hear of students not completing the course successfully, but unfortunately it happens!).

No one (including you) has to fear spending an eternity in hell if you have placed your faith in Jesus Christ to save your soul (see the chapter on "Salvation"). On the contrary, it is a very real place that is the consequence of those who choose not to place their trust in Jesus Christ to save their soul. Hell is only experienced by those who choose to reject Jesus Christ's offer of salvation for their sins.

A profound reality
Unfortunately, the word "hell" is relegated to a vain word that is carelessly used during times of anger or frustration. It is referenced without real purpose or understanding that hell is a real, authentic place. According to God's Word, hell is more than a curse word—it is a self-chosen destiny for some.

Remember, the reason anyone will experience hell is because of their choices to: (1) not acknowledge their sinfulness and need for forgiveness; (2) not desire to submit to the authority of God in confession of their sin; (3) not trust the reality of the Deity of Jesus Christ and His atoning work to provide salvation for sin. Hell is a horrific byproduct of choice not to acknowledge God's truth regarding one's spiritual condition.

Open your mouth
The reality of hell should cause all believers to open their mouths to share the invitation of God's saving grace that is offered to the world. It should motivate those who themselves have been saved from the consequences of their sin to desire for others to also have peace with God.

Watch and learn
I think of all the literal, physical and horrific characteristics of hell, one of the most torturous characteristics will be that everyone who takes their eternal residence in hell will retain their memory. As with the description in Luke 16, the account ends with the man recalling the truth he had heard about the need to follow God and believe His Word. In his agony he begs that someone would go and warn his living loved ones.

Here are some practical ways the reality of hell can motivate you to progress in your spiritual walk today:

1. Don't watch the clock
Let the reality of hell motivate you to take the extra time to talk to your

unsaved family and friends about their need for salvation. While people take this encouragement to heart, it is important to remember to allow the powerful truth of the Word of God to speak for itself. Unfortunately, some become ineffective messengers because their presentation of the gospel is not clear. Practice how you will explain the key points of salvation, and allow the reality of hell to cause you to boldly share the gospel story with those who need to hear it (Romans 1:16).

2. Don't fear what once was—but glory in what is now

Even though hell is a real, physical, eternal state for those who do not trust in God to save their souls, if you have put your trust in Him, you have been redeemed from your sins (see the chapter on "Salvation")—now you should glory in your salvation! Never forget what God did for you, but focus now on your eternal promise that one day you will be in heaven eternally with Him. Even in Ephesians 2:1-11, after describing the horrific state of our sinful souls, Paul turns the corner at verse four and begins to change our focus toward the great salvation that God has provided every believer.

3. Never become desensitized to the reality of hell

It is a real place where real people go if they do not make the real decision to accept Christ as their personal Savior. If you have a loved one who has not accepted Christ, never stop praying for him/her. If you know of co-workers that need to accept the Lord Jesus Christ, begin to passionately pray for them and find the courage to talk to them about their need for salvation. And remember, don't get angry at a person who is hostile with you regarding your Christianity. Rather, feel pity for those souls and pray passionately for their future salvation. May we never become desensitized to others' need for salvation.

Study what the Bible says about hell

Here are some more verses to read on this topic—Matthew 11:21-24; Revelation 20:14-15; Romans 6:23; Matthew 25.

Write it down... ⇢

...& make it HAPPEN!

CONCLUSION:
CONTINUE ON YOUR SPIRITUAL JOURNEY

One February morning my father and I donned our heaviest winter coats and headed to the state park to go hiking in the thick deep snow. I knew we had veered off of the path because I found the soul of my boot slipping out from under me more so than earlier in the day. Knowing something was different, I stopped for a moment, and with my boot I began to scratch away at the snow underneath me, in hopes of finding dirt and dead grass. What I discovered was that we were standing on a solid, dark, frozen sheet of ice. Instantly, I looked up and I looked all around me in order to get my bearings. "We're on the lake, Dad!"

I began to get scared as thoughts of cracking through the ice in sub-freezing weather shot through my young mind. I remember asking my father a very important question, "Are we safe, Dad?!" To which he replied, "If it's frozen all the way through, we'll be okay." Immediately, I was not convinced because his statement started with the word "IF." I wanted to know for sure! There was no way I wanted to fall into the icy waters to get my answer—I wanted to know for sure.

At that moment, my dad pointed ahead of us and said, "Look!" In the distance we saw an ice fisherman with a tent, sitting on a stool and fishing. "See him," Dad said. "It must be safe because he's out here too." Even though it was nice to see another person putting their faith in the ice and believing it would hold his weight—it was not enough to go on. I still wasn't sure if I was going to be swimming in sub-freezing water. Just knowing someone else believed the ice was thick enough to hold him wasn't good enough for me. I needed to know it would hold me for sure.

Just then, all my questions and fears subsided when I saw a huge, heavy black pick-up truck driving across the lake. It was HUGE! I had never seen that occur before—a huge truck just cruisin' across a lake! It was an odd sight, and I just stared in amazement as it drove by. Right then I found myself laughing at the sight! We needed to stop and allow a two-ton truck to drive by us on a frozen lake. How bizarre! But I also laughed out of relief because now I was confident that I had nothing to worry about. It was finally demonstrated to me that this ice really could support my weight, my father's weight, the weight of the ice fisherman, and that two-ton truck racing on the ice in front of us! My father turned around with a smile and said, "I think we're okay!"

We hope that this book has shown you that you can trust Jesus Christ and

His Holy Word—you can base your life on Him. We trust you have received and understood the basic foundation for Christianity, and you are confident that you are standing on a firm foundation when you place your faith in Jesus Christ. We encourage you to continue to engage in spiritual discussion with other believers, to read and meditate on God's Word and to pray and ask God to teach you more about Him. It will be the most rewarding thing you've ever done in your life.

Our prayers will constantly be with you as you continue on your spiritual journey!

REFERENCES

References throughout the book include the following sources:

Elwell, W. A. (2001). Evangelical Dictionary of Theology (2nd ed.). Grand Rapids: Baker Academic.

Erickson, M. J. (1998). Christian Theology (2nd ed.). Grand Rapids: Baker Academic.

Grenz, S. J., Guretzki, D., & Nordling, C. F. (1999). Pocket Dictionary of Theological Terms. Downers Grove: IVP Academic.

Grudem, W., & Purswell, J. (1999). Bible Doctrine (Abridged.). Zondervan.

Spurgeon, C.H. (June 20, 1858).Sermon delivered at the Music Hall, Royal Surrey Gardens. www.spurgeon.org/sermons/0201.htm.

The ESV Study Bible. (2008). (1st ed.). Wheaton, IL: Crossway Bibles.

Tozer, A. W. (1961). The Knowledge of the Holy: The Attributes of God, Their Meaning in the Christian Life (1st ed.). San Francisco: Harper & Row.

Vine, W. E., Unger, M., & White, W. (1985). Vine's Complete Expository Dictionary of Old and New Testament Words. Nashville, TN: Thomas Nelson Publishers.

Warren, R. (2002). The Purpose Driven Life (1st ed.). Grand Rapids, MI: Zondervan.

Zacharias, R. (2010). Beyond Opinion: Living the Faith We Defend (Reprint.). Nashville: Thomas Nelson.

ABOUT THE AUTHORS

DR. GABRIEL ETZEL is the Associate Dean for the School of Religion at Liberty University. He is also an Associate Professor of Religion and has been on faculty at Liberty University since 2004. In addition, he actively serves as a Life Group leader at Thomas Road Baptist Church in Lynchburg, VA. Dr. Etzel double-majored in Finance and Biblical Literature at Indiana Wesleyan University, where he received his Bachelor of Science degree. He then attended Liberty Baptist Theological Seminary and completed a Master of Arts in Religion, Master of Divinity, and Doctor of Ministry degrees. He is currently pursuing a PhD in Leadership from The Southern Baptist Theological Seminary in Louisville, KY. Dr. Etzel and his wife Whitney have three children, Landon, Ava and Isaac, and reside in Lynchburg, Virginia.

DR. BEN GUTIERREZ is Professor of Religion at Liberty University in Lynchburg, Virginia. He also serves as an Associate Pastor of Thomas Road Baptist Church. Dr. Gutierrez received a Diploma from Word of Life Bible Institute, and AA and BS in Religion from Liberty University, a Master of Arts in Religion and a Master of Divinity from Liberty Baptist Theological Seminary, and PhD from Regent University. He is the co-author of Learn to Read New Testament Greek Workbook (2009) published by Broadman and Holman, an excellent resource to supplement one's study of the Koine Greek language; co-author of Ministry Is: How to serve Jesus with Passion and Confidence (2010) published by Broadman and Holman, a practical guide on how to serve effectively in the local church; and co-editor of the The Essence of the New Testament: A Survey (2012) published by Broadman and Holman, a thorough, readable survey of the New Testament that includes introductions, background information, outlines, archaeological facts, theological concepts, word studies, study questions and practical applications. Dr. Gutierrez and his wife Tammy have two daughters, Lauren and Emma, and reside in Lynchburg, Virginia.